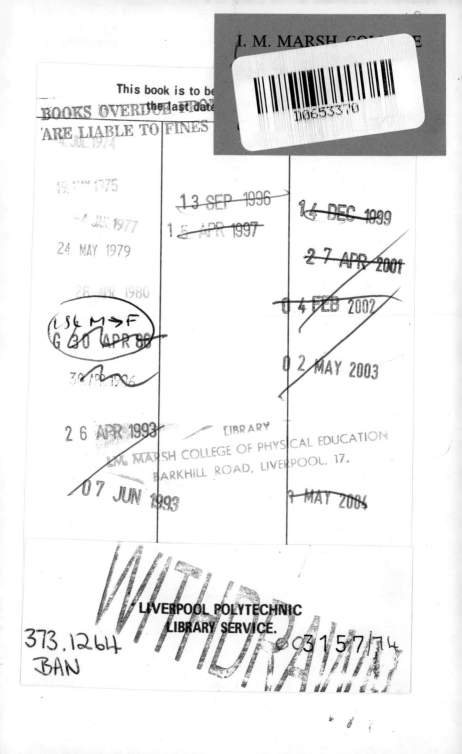

SUCCESS AND FAILURE IN THE SECONDARY SCHOOL:

**An interdisciplinary approach
to school achievement**

SUCCESS AND FAILURE IN THE SECONDARY SCHOOL:
An interdisciplinary approach
to school achievement

OLIVE BANKS AND DOUGLAS FINLAYSON

METHUEN & CO LTD
11 NEW FETTER LANE, LONDON EC4

First published by Methuen & Co. Ltd
11 New Fetter Lane, London EC4

© *1973 Olive Banks and Douglas Finlayson*

Printed in Great Britain by
Cox & Wyman Ltd, Fakenham, Norfolk

SBN (hardbound) 416 76440 1
SBN (paperback) 416 76450 9

Distributed in the USA by
HARPER & ROW PUBLISHERS INC.
BARNES & NOBLE IMPORT DIVISON

CONTENTS

PREFACE

This book grew out of a feeling of unease shared by the two authors about the nature of much of the educational research which has been done in relation to the problem of school achievement. It is appropriate therefore that we should make explicit at the very beginning of the book the bases of our unease.

The first was our concern in 1964 at the lack of understanding which many psychologists and sociologists displayed of the other's point of view in their published work on school achievement. Their respective contributions to the debate on secondary reorganization and the role of the 11-plus examination illustrated well the extent of the division between them. Taking the view that co-operation between the disciplines in relation to school achievement was likely to be more productive than hostility the planning of a joint study of the problem was begun in that year.

The second was the shared belief that the current level of understanding of the complexities of the social process of which school achievement is but one outcome falls far short of what is desirable. In a competitive society where the level of achievement in school has associated with it many important and lasting vocational and financial consequences for individuals, this point is of special significance for those concerned about the inequality of opportunity which has so often been demonstrated in that competition, and about the short-term emotional costs which failure at school may involve for some individuals.

The third is a belief that, lacking understanding of the process of school achievement, large-scale statistical exercises of a predictive nature, as were undertaken for the Plowden Committee, were perhaps premature. To have an appropriate methodology available to perform these predictive exercises is a necessary condition but certainly not a sufficient reason for their performance. The 'answers' they produce add little to our understanding of the complexities of the process about which they are predicting and may unwittingly serve to divert attention away from some aspects of the process to which attention requires to be drawn.

In the light of these beliefs, it might be said that we were inconsistent to use a predictive instrument, namely an 11-plus battery of tests and teachers' assessments, to select the main groups of parents and pupils for our study. There is however no inconsistency, for our interest is in those pupils whose actual academic performance differed most from their predicted performance. By studying children whose performance the predictors failed to predict, we are not accepting prediction but focusing on the 'error component' of an educational selection procedure of known efficiency. We are not dismissing this 'error component' as due to random effects, but treating it as a dependent variable so that factors associated with it can be identified. In this way, we are regarding the 'error component' as representing the margin of variability in achievement, which may be open to influence by parents and teachers, at the secondary stage given the present educational situation.

By accepting this situation, its organizational features, its emphasis on achievement and current teacher, parent-pupil beliefs we may be regarded as reactionary and 'unprogressive' by those who subscribe to certain ideological positions. But we make no apology for our concern with what is rather than what ought to be. By adopting this viewpoint we hope that the book will make an empirical, as distinct from an ideological, contribution to an understanding of the problem of social inequality in relation to school achievement.

Because of the widespread interest in our topic, we have tried to produce a book that is both popular and academic. For the benefit of the latter audience, all the statistical justifications for our discussion have been gathered together and presented in an appendix. For the less specialized audience as few technical terms as possible have been used, and only those tables that are either readily understandable or critical to our argument are presented in the text. Where possible, the findings have been illustrated using case study material which emphasizes the human aspects of the achievement process.

We have to acknowledge the help we received from many sources. The Department of Education and Science financed the initial research but the views expressed in this book are entirely the authors' own responsibility. We also wish to acknowledge the co-operation and help of the officers of the local authority who allowed us access to their records and to their schools. A special acknowledgement is due to the headmasters, members of staff and pupils of the three schools whose co-operation was continually forthcoming over the period of three years when we were in and out of their classrooms, and to the parents of the boys who were so ready to answer all the questions we asked them, to discuss with us all the problems we raised, and who provided us with so many cups of tea or coffee.

During the course of the study we were particularly indebted to Mr Wilf Connor, Mrs Jane Forster and Mrs Cynthia Jones who collected and processed much of our data, to Mr Alan Kirk for his help in the analysis of our data, to Dr W. Robinson for his advice on the assessment of the achievement motive, to Linden Hilgendorf and Barry Irving with whom we discussed the hierarchical analysis procedure, and to Terry Pitt, Valerie Owen and Ann Brown for typing the manuscript.

O.B.
D.S.F.

ACKNOWLEDGEMENTS

The authors and publishers would like to thank the *British Journal of Educational Psychology* for permission to reproduce Tables A3.2–3, on p. 222, and *Research in Education* for permission to reproduce Figure 7.1, and Table A7.4 on p. 243.

CHAPTER ONE

TOWARDS AN UNDERSTANDING OF SCHOOL ACHIEVEMENT

I THE BACKGROUND

The fact of differences in school achievement, and the search for an explanation of those differences, is one of the most complex and, at the present time, one of the most controversial issues in education today. It has been the focus of numerous researches and the topic of many government reports, not only in this country, but in most of the industrialized and industrializing countries of the world. Yet in spite of an impressive bibliography we are still almost as far from reaching an understanding of the actual process of school achievement as we were ten years ago.

This is not to suggest that research has been altogether inconclusive. Although a detailed review of findings would be out of place here, such factors as parents' socio-economic status, family size, aspirations of both parents and children, and characteristics of the child such as ability, motivation and some personality traits have all been shown to be associated with school achievement in a wide variety of contexts. Moreover, in recent years a number of studies have attempted to assess the relative importance of these and other factors. In this country, for example, the Plowden Report[1] attempted to differentiate the effect of

[1] Report of the Central Advisory Council for Education (England), *Children and their Primary Schools* (London, HMSO, 1967).

home circumstances, including the physical amenities, the number of dependent children and parents' education, from the effect of parental attitudes and from the effect of the school. Similarly Coleman,[1] in a study undertaken on behalf of the US Office of Education, looked at the relative contribution of a number of aspects of the school. On the whole, however, most studies have been content to demonstrate a relationship between one, or a small number of variables and school achievement, and even when a multidimensional approach has been used the range of variables has been restricted.

Perhaps the most serious weakness of a great deal of research in this field is that it has failed to look in more than a superficial way at the actual process of school failure or school success. In consequence we are left all too often with a statistical relationship or a series of relationships but no understanding of the causal sequences among the factors involved. Even a longitudinal study, like the extensive survey carried out by Douglas and his associates,[2] includes very little information that could be used in this way.

This is not to imply that no studies exist which are concerned with the description of school achievement as an ongoing process. An early study by Jackson and Marsden[3] provides a very detailed account of a group of working-class boys who had passed successfully through grammar school. This is a vivid study full of insights but it has several weaknesses, of which perhaps the most important is the long period of time that necessarily intervened between the interviews and the experiences they describe. There are also faults in the design of the study which seriously limit the inferences that can be drawn from it.

The recent account by Lacey in his intensive study of a single

[1] J. S. Coleman, *Equality of Educational Opportunity* (USOE, GPO, 1966).
[2] J. W. B. Douglas, *The Home and the School* (London, MacGibbon and Kee, 1964).
[3] B. Jackson and D. Marsden, *Education and the Working Class* (London, Routledge and Kegan Paul, 1962).

grammar school[1] also makes use of a model which is quite explicitly concerned with achievement as a process involving what he terms differentiation and polarization. By differentiation Lacey means the separation and ranking of students, largely carried out by teachers in the course of their normal duties, in accordance with the academically orientated value system of the grammar school. Such ranking will include assessments of behaviour as well as of school work. Polarization, on the other hand, takes place within the student body, although it is affected by the process of differentiation. A boy who does badly academically is predisposed to reject the system which has placed him in an inferior position, and in extreme situations an anti-school culture may develop. Successful boys are predisposed to accept the culture of the school. His analysis takes the form of a longitudinal study, and includes a number of case studies designed to illustrate the relationship between the home, the school and the achievement of the child. In so far as this is primarily a study of a school, however, the material on home background is limited in extent. On the whole, therefore, in spite of these and other similar studies, the highly complex and dynamic pattern of relationships which underlies differences in school achievement is still inadequately described and little understood.

A further problem is the need, in any explanatory theory in this field, to come to some understanding of the relationship between social structure and personality, which itself implies an interdisciplinary approach involving psychology, social psychology and sociology. In spite of the apparent desirability of such a co-operative endeavour there have been few attempts, particularly in this country, to translate such an aim into concrete terms. This is not to say that at times both psychologists and sociologists have not made use of each other's concepts and techniques, but this borrowing has rarely involved a genuinely interdisciplinary approach in which the relationship between psychological and sociological explanations of school achievement could be examined in a systematic way. Such an approach,

[1] C. Lacey, *Hightown Grammar* (Manchester, Manchester University Press, 1970).

it is true, involves many difficulties in communication between those trained in separate disciplines, employing not only different concepts but alternative techniques of research. There is also the problem of handling a great volume of material representing a wide variety of kinds of data and, furthermore, integrating the findings in a way that is meaningful to both disciplines without falling into a form of reductionism in which sociology disappears into psychology or psychology into sociology.

Arising out of the authors' common belief that an interdisciplinary approach towards the understanding of school achievement was necessary, the Department of Education and Science (as it now is) was approached for the necessary financial support. Subsequently a joint project was initiated which, it was hoped, would enable us to extend our understanding of the actual process whereby a child living in a particular home comes to achieve or fail to achieve in school.

The project was designed, it must be emphasized, not with the intention of providing any definitive answers to the many difficult questions which abound in this area, but rather to seek to provide some kind of framework within which some of the complexities of the process of which school achievement is but one outcome can be conceptualized. This formulation, it was hoped, would provide a basis for later larger-scale systematic research to test specific hypotheses that might be derived from the conceptual structure.

Although limited in its aims, an interdisciplinary project of this nature would necessarily involve at the individual level the collection of a great amount of data, both from pupils and their parents. With only two fieldworkers available, certain crucial decisions regarding basic design, sampling and methods of analysis were necessary in the early stages of the project. Every such decision was difficult, for it brought with it consequences whose effects would be carried forward into the later stages of the study. Another difficulty was that a number of these decisions had to be made with only a limited amount of information available beforehand and only after the research data had been collected did the full consequences of some of these decisions emerge. The extent of some of those consequences will be made explicit later, but the kind of problems which presented themselves can be illustrated in relation to the school factor.

Because we were concerned to take into account variations in the school itself, since this is the social context within which success or failure takes place, this ruled out the study of a single school. But, given the limitation of our resources, it was decided to restrict the number of schools studied to three. This would allow some within- and between-school comparisons to be made but would not stretch our resources too thinly to make an adequate study of each school. For the same reason girls were excluded from our study, since previous work had suggested that the process of school achievement in the case of girls is not only different from boys but may even be more complex.

The selection of the three schools presented the team with considerable difficulty as it naturally involved decisions with respect to the age, ability and social background of the children, decisions moreover which had to some extent to be arbitrary since by focusing on one area we were perforce neglecting others. In the event it was decided to concentrate on the secondary stage and to look at school achievement in the particular context of the selective school. The choice of such a programme in spite of the possible alternatives seemed to have several merits. In the first place grammar school success and failure had been the subject of several recent studies which provided us with guidelines for our own researches. In addition it enabled us to focus on boys following roughly similar courses and, although in different schools, preparing for the same external examinations.

One of the schools was a traditional grammar school with a distinguished record of Oxford and Cambridge scholarship successes, and another a grammar technical school which had until recently been a technical school of long standing. The third choice introduced further variation since it was a new comprehensive school which at the time of our study was organized into three 'blocks' according to academic ability. The ablest 'block' followed a course of study comparable to that of the two selective schools and only boys in this 'academic' block were included in our sample. This school unlike the other was coeducational, but the girls were not included in the study. The three schools chosen for study were therefore very different in their traditions, and this was reflected in their entrance halls and corridors. In the grammar school the walls of the entrance hall were covered by large oak panels bearing the dated academic honours won by former pupils. In the entrance to the grammar technical school stood a fairly small glass exhibition case in which were displayed, from time to time, examples of high precision engineering craftsmanship which the pupils had produced. In the comprehensive school large glass exhibition cases containing sporting and other trophies were very much in evidence, and pictures, many painted by the children, and other works of art were liberally displayed.

There were also several interesting differences in the way the schools were organized. In the traditional grammar school, streaming into express and non-express forms was instituted at the end of the first year, when the boys also had to choose between an emphasis on science or on arts subjects. Partly because of its academic emphasis and partly because it was housed in old restrictive buildings, facilities for sport and for non-academic subjects were limited. The grammar technical school by contrast was new and well equipped. On the other hand, because it originated as a technical high school it had a bias towards scientific and technical rather than linguistic subjects, and it did not have the same reputation for academic success. Unlike the traditional grammar school, teaching was in mixed ability groups for the first two years, after which some limited streaming was introduced, and there was no express stream. The comprehensive school was also new and well equipped, with excellent facilities for non-academic subjects and courses. The academic block, however, was treated very much as a unit by the school, at least for academic purposes. Streaming and setting within the block were introduced from the start, and were taken seriously by both the boys and their parents, movement from one stream to another being perceived as movement 'up' or 'down'. By choosing these particular schools, therefore, we hoped to introduce some variation in the school setting while retaining a higher degree of comparability than if the whole range of pupil ability had been included in the sample.

This particular feature of our research design did, however, introduce several problems which complicated our research and which have implications for the generality of our findings. In the large northern industrial town where the study took place, the 11-plus procedure included parental choice with no zoning qualifications. Parents were invited to list several schools in order of preference and boys were allocated to schools according to their total 11-plus quotient score, the boy with the highest score being granted the school of his parents' first choice, and so on down the list. Thus the higher the 11-plus score, the more likely it was that parents would receive their first choice of school, whereas those in the borderline category might be allocated to a school low on their parents' list, or not even on the list at all.

The operation of this system resulted in the traditional grammar school with its distinguished reputation receiving boys of the highest ability, since such was its popularity that only boys with high 11-plus scores could hope for a place. Indeed it was able to 'cream' primary schools all over the city. The comprehensive school by contrast had at that time little reputation among parents, so that it received only boys of 'borderline' ability. The technical grammar school had a high reputation in its immediate area because of its attractive buildings. It was also popular with those parents who wanted a technical bias in the education of their sons. Consequently it was able to attract pupils of higher ability as measured by the 11-plus procedure than was the comprehensive school. For the intake of boys who formed the subjects of our study, the 11-plus quotient mean for the traditional grammar school was 740·45 (n = 174), for the technical grammar school 689·54 (n = 90) and for the comprehensive school 638·32 (n = 81). One-way analysis of variance gave a highly significant F ratio when the differences between these scores were tested for statistical significance, thus indicating that the three schools represented different strata of pupil ability. Indeed, for this particular intake, those with

the lowest scores at the traditional grammar school had
similar scores to the very ablest boys at the comprehensive
school.

Table 1.1 *Range of 11-plus quotient scores*

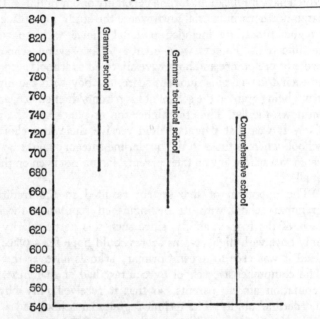

A random sample of parents, interviewed during the course of
the boy's first year at the school, revealed that the difference
between the schools with respect to pupil ability as measured by
11-plus quotients was repeated in a number of measures of
socio-economic status and other parental characteristics. These
differences, which are crucial to the interpretation of our findings, will be described in more detail later, but some of the more
important can be indicated briefly at this point. For example,
the traditional grammar school had the highest proportion of
pupils from non-manual families and the comprehensive school
the lowest, with the technical grammar school, again, in the

intermediate position. Parental incomes were also higher in the traditional grammar school than in either of the other schools, and parents at this school were also more likely to be house owners. Family size was also significantly larger at the comprehensive school than at the other two schools. In addition there were some differences in aspirations, with parents and boys having higher aspirations at the traditional grammar school.

The causes of these differences are complex, and the differences in ability are clearly related to differences in the reputation of the schools concerned. The effect, however, has been to maximize the differences between pupils and their parents *between* schools and to minimize such differences *within* schools. In consequence a number of the factors which are generally associated with school achievement, although they are found as differences between our schools, are not and indeed in some cases cannot be closely associated with achievement within a school. A particularly striking example is the homogeneity of the comprehensive school with respect to socio-economic status and its associated variables. This is, in effect, a working-class school, so that differences in achievement in this school cannot be explained in terms of social class. In the traditional grammar school, conversely, although there are marked differences in the socioeconomic status of the parents, they are nevertheless very similar to each other in their interest in education and their aspirations for their sons. At the same time it becomes very difficult to compare the effect of different school contexts, since the pupils themselves differed so much between schools. The differences in ability alone mean that comparisons between the effect of the traditional grammar school and the comprehensive in particular can be made for only a small proportion of the pupils if the effect of differences in ability is to be controlled. Similarly, in comparing these two schools it must always be remembered that there are differences not only in the school context but in the social class background of a large number of the pupils. The limitations, as well as certain advantages, of this aspect of our study will be discussed in more detail with reference to particular findings.

2 THE SAMPLES

Since the emphasis was to be on the *process* of achievement it was decided to follow through a particular group of boys in each school for as long as our resources permitted. Accordingly, the whole of the first year's intake in the two grammar schools, and all the boys entering the first year of the academic block in the comprehensive school, formed the core of the study. This gave us a total of 345 boys, 174 in the traditional grammar, 90 in the technical grammar and 81 in the comprehensive school. Results of the 11-plus procedure for these boys were made available to us by the local education authority, and further tests were given over a period of four years. In addition we collected information from the schools on the boys' performance in the internal examinations held at the end of the first, second and third years. At a later stage we were given access to their GCE results. During the four years of the study the boys also filled in a large number of questionnaires on a variety of topics. This particular group will be referred to as the main sample.

From this main sample we selected two other sub-samples for more intensive study. The first of these was a stratified random sample drawn[1] from the main sample in each of the three schools at the beginning of the first school year, and was composed of 132 boys, 47 from the traditional grammar school, 46 from the technical grammar school and 39 from the comprehensive school. Although of occasional use in the collection of certain information which it was not practicable to obtain from the main sample, its main purpose was to enable us to select for interview a small group of parents in order to provide us with a background of knowledge on the similarities and differences between parents in the three schools. Apart from questions on economic circumstances, educational background, and values and aspirations, we were interested in such topics as experience of the primary school, the transition to secondary education and expectations of the new school. The answers to these questions and the lengthy discussions which sometimes followed gave us

[1] For the details of how this sample was drawn see appendix 1, p. 193.

not only specific responses to particular questions but a great deal of general information, particularly on the way in which parents perceived the educational process, which was to be useful in framing the questions in further phases of the study.

Interviewing began in November 1964 and was completed in the following spring. A preliminary letter was sent to each family in the sample, outlining the nature of the research, and this was followed by a visit to arrange an interview at a time when both parents could be present. Consideration was given to the possibility of arranging separate interviews with mothers and fathers but this was ruled out as both too timeconsuming and too difficult to arrange. Although this joint interview had many disadvantages, it did enable us to observe the parents together, and in a large number of cases the posing of the questions sparked off an argument between the parents which provided us with useful extra information. In most cases, when contacted, parents proved co-operative and 127 interviews were completed out of a possible total of 132, although it was often difficult to make the first contact, particularly when both parents were at work.

This particular phase of the project did however involve a considerable expenditure of time and effort. Since almost all the interviews had to take place in the evening and since parents tended to ask for a mid-evening appointment it was rarely possible to fit two interviews into one day. There were also a number of broken appointments and a second and in some cases a third appointment had to be made. As a result of our experiences, our plans for further parental interviews were scaled down, since our resources in terms of time and staff were limited. Undoubtedly our task would have been easier if we had been satisfied to interview the mothers only, but the inclusion of the fathers was an intrinsic part of the research design, and they were included in every phase of our interviewing programme. It was with great regret that we decided that our resources would not allow us to interview the random sample of parents again, for a comparison of changes in their attitudes and aspirations over time would have been immensely valuable. So that we would have some comparative information, the parents were contacted a year later by means of a postal questionnaire, but the response rate was disappointing and it was not repeated in subsequent years.

In addition a further thirty boys were selected from within this sample. These boys were randomly selected from those within each school whose IQ scores fell into the group 110–19 and so provided us with a small number of boys of similar IQ within each school for the purpose of a comparison between schools in the light of GCE results when these became available. The parents of these boys were interviewed along with the rest of the main sample during the first year and again in the second year. The original plan to reinterview them again in the fourth year had to be abandoned because of lack of time.

Although these interviews of parents were of value to the study in that they provided a backcloth against which other data in the project could be viewed, the main focus was on the factors associated with differential success in school achievement. Given the relative homogeneity of the within-school population it was felt that a study of extreme groups, rather than a random sample, would be more likely to provide data which would serve our purpose. Accordingly, two groups were selected for intensive study – one of high achieving and one of poorly achieving boys. These two groups will be termed, for the sake of brevity and convenience, the successful and the unsuccessful boys, but it is important at the outset to define as precisely as possible what we mean by these terms. This is a difficult exercise in view of the fact that schools are supposed to be concerned with many aspects of a child's progress, although some of these tend to be rather vaguely defined and difficult to assess, e.g. social development. Because of the already heavy load being undertaken by the research team, it was felt to be impossible to consider any aspect of success which could not be readily assessed. Therefore success in this study is defined in terms of school achievement. This approach would also appear to be justified in so far as it is the context in which most of the discussion of and research into school success has been placed.

Even after limiting the concept of success specifically to school achievement, however, further problems arise in deciding on the actual criteria to be used for this purpose. High and low academic achievement can of course be defined quite simply in terms of some standard of performance based on results in attainment tests or school examinations, but individual differences in ability and aptitude will contribute substantially to the results which pupils produce in such tests or examinations. If other influences are to be examined then some control over ability is necessary. This could have been achieved by matching pupils for ability and then selecting paired groups of high and low achievers, but this method raises doubts if groups from different schools, between which there are significant differences in ability, are to be combined. Alternatively some form of ranking of pupils might have been employed on ability and attainment measures. From these rankings pupils who were higher or lower in attainment, relative to their ability ranking, could have been designated over- and under-achievers respectively. The limitation of this latter procedure is that it fails to take account of the phenomenon of regression and so seriously minimizes the number of over-attainers of high ability and the number of under-attainers of low ability. Moreover the terms under-achievement and particularly over-achievement are vague and even misleading unless defined precisely.

The solution finally adopted was to define success and unsuccess operationally in terms of the discrepancy between *actual* attainment and *predicted* attainment, which is estimated from the regression equation between aptitude or predicted attainment and observed attainment. Success or 'over-achievement' is said to occur when the actual attainment exceeds the predicted attainment, and failure or 'under-achievement' when the actual attainment drops below the predicted level. The use of such a statistical criterion has the added advantage that 'under' and 'over' achievement in different examinations within the same school, and in examinations in different schools, can be expressed in comparable terms.

The measure of predicted achievement finally decided on was the combined 11-plus battery made up of standardized tests of verbal reasoning, English and arithmetic and primary school teachers' scaled estimates, these having equal weighting with the three standardized tests. In making use of this measure it is not intended to imply that it is in any sense a measure of innate or potential ability. Indeed this or any other measure must of necessity be the result of the interaction between a hypothesized innate predisposition and the effect of a particular environment. It has been demonstrated[1] however that a measure of this kind is the best predictor we have of future school achievement as defined by success in the GCE examination. Put in another way we may say that performance in the 11-plus is a measure of the level of achievement reached by the child at the end of the primary school stage, and that this summary of past achievement is the best predictor we have of future achievement. The child who significantly improves upon his earlier performance or who significantly falls below it is therefore of considerable theoretical and practical interest. It seems likely that an intensive study of these children and their background will highlight those factors which may be said to be favourable for school achievement in a particular school context, and those which appear to hinder it.

The measurement of school achievement itself was an even more difficult problem, since standardized tests of attainment, even where available, were extremely restricted in their content. Consequently end-of-session examinations for each of the first three years in each of the schools were used. Different combinations of subjects occurred between schools and years, but no objection was taken to this, as it was the overall effect of various factors, rather than their effect on particular subjects, with which the study was concerned.

In most of the subjects one common paper was given to all classes and the scripts were marked by the same markers throughout. In subjects where this was not done the marks were scaled using the combined 11-plus quotient total as the common measure. The marks were standardized within each school separately, using units which caused as little disturbance to the original scores as possible, and the subjects weighted in terms of the amount of timetable they received. Three achieve-

[1] A. Yates and D. Pidgeon, *Admission to Grammar Schools* (London, Newnes, 1957).

ment scores for each boy were obtained by summing across subjects in each examination.

The method used to select the groups of successful and unsuccessful boys is described in detail in appendix 2.[1] Briefly, however, the standard error of the predictions made from each regression equation was calculated so that the degree of confidence associated with the magnitude of particular differences between the predicted and actual scores could be indicated. Those pupils for whom the difference between their actual and predicted scores fell within the limits of the probable error (50 per cent of the year group) were regarded as achieving as expected, while those whose actual achievement exceeded their predicted score by more than the probable error were regarded as over-achievers, and those whose actual acheivement fell below their predicted acheivement by more than the probable error were regarded as under-acheivers.

In order to select from within these two groups of successful and unsuccessful boys, we started from the extremes of over- and under-achievement as we had defined them, and continued until two similarly sized groups of from ten to twelve boys were obtained in each school. Boys who did not live with their parents or who did not have both parents alive were excluded, and so were a few boys who were unusual in that no 11-plus data were available or who were repeating a year because of illness. These groups of successful and unsuccessful boys were selected at two different times during the project. The first occasion was at the end of the first year, on the basis of the first year examination results only, and the second was at the end of the third year, based on the cumulative scores over the three years.

Although parents were interviewed during the boys' second year, using the first year groups, the main thrust of the analysis was on the groups selected on the basis of the boys' cumulative performance. The parents of these boys were interviewed during the boys' fourth year at the school. To some extent these two groups of boys overlapped, as some boys started to 'over-achieve' or 'under-achieve' in the first year and maintained this pattern subsequently. In other cases the pattern was broken and

[1] See pp. 196–8.

'over-achievers' or successful boys failed to maintain their progress, and 'under-achievers' or unsuccessful boys recovered from their initial setback. Table 1.2 sets out the number of boys whose parents were in each category in both the first and third year success/unsuccess categories, and also indicates the extent to which the two groups overlapped. Altogether just over 60 per cent of the boys included in the success/unsuccess group in the first year also appear in the third year groups but exact comparisons are not possible because the numbers differ in each of the school year groups.

Ideally we would have liked to reinterview the parents of the boys who were no longer in the success/unsuccess category at the end of the third year, but our resources did not allow this. Not only had the interviews proved very costly in time and energy, but the coding of the second year interviews had also proved more complicated than we had expected owing to the large amount of data collected, so that we were running behind schedule. To add to our problems, we were without one of our two research workers during this particular year. Consequently we did not interview any of the parents of boys who were no longer in the success/unsuccess category.

In the main, parents once they had agreed to the interview were co-operative but there were occasional problems which

Table 1.2 *Comparison of first and third year successful and unsuccessful groups*

School	1st year group	3rd year group	No. in both groups	No. in 3rd year but not in 1st year
Traditional grammar	24	20	13	7
Grammar technical	22	21	12	9
Comprehensive	18	21	13	8
Total	64	62	38	24

had not occurred during the much simpler interviews carried out with the random sample during the first year. Part of the difficulty arose from the length of the interview, which lasted on average two to three hours but in some instances stretched to four hours. Most of these long sessions were enjoyed by the parents but occasionally an interview touched on an area of great personal anxiety and in a few cases the parents became very distressed. Situations of this kind tended to occur when the boy was doing very badly at school, and one of the strongest impressions retained of the interviews as a whole is the extent to which these parents were emotionally involved in their son's progress at school.

Outright refusals were rare, and in the case of the first year group we interviewed the parents of sixty-two boys out of a possible total of sixty-four. In the case of the third year group interviews were more difficult to arrange, possibly reflecting less interest as the boys grew older. Parents who had already been interviewed were also unwilling in many cases to be seen a second time. In fact we obtained some information from the parents of fifty-eight out of a possible sixty-one boys but not all these interviews were complete.

3 THE RESEARCH PROCEDURE

Within the limitations of our resources the emphasis in the collection of data was on comprehensiveness. This approach was necessitated by our predilection for an interdisciplinary approach, by our interest in achievement as a continuous process rather than in the effect of particular factors or variables, and by our choice of an intensive study of a small number of specially selected families, rather than a sample survey design. This meant that we gathered information over a very wide range, including, for the boys, measures of personality, motivation, beliefs and values, interests and activities. In the case of the parents we included not only measures of socio-economic status, including educational background and the material aspects of the home, but also a series of questions on aspirations and values and on patterns of child-rearing.

The result was inevitably a very large amount of data both for the groups of boys as a whole and for the families in our samples. The data too were very varied in their nature, ranging from questionnaires to ratings of child-rearing patterns and the emotional atmosphere of the home. This meant that no common pattern could be adopted for the analysis of the data. Although for some of the material a purely descriptive procedure could have been followed, this would not have allowed us to examine the interrelationship between different kinds of variables, except in a purely impressionistic way. Consequently a procedure was devised which allowed us to handle the large amount of data and reduce them to manageable form. Fundamentally, this involved a prior quantification in the form of scores or ratings and subsequently a grouping into clusters on the basis of statistical as well as conceptual relationships. Details of this procedure are outlined in appendix 3,[1] and it will also be described briefly in the relevant sections of subsequent chapters. As an approach it has the advantage that, although the descriptive case studies are available and will be drawn upon frequently, a more precise examination of particular interrelationships is also possible.

The presentation of findings that has been adopted here follows to some extent from the method of analysis. Starting from the personality of the pupil himself, successive chapters consider motivation, patterns of child-rearing and the socio-economic status of the family in terms of their relationship to school achievement. A subsequent chapter examines ways in which these various attributes of the boy and aspects of his family background are interrelated in the process of achievement. Finally, we look at the effect of different school contexts on achievement and consider some of the educational implications of our findings in general.

Before presenting the findings, however, an attempt should be made to indicate some of the hazards of interpreting the results of a study of this kind. It has already been suggested that the choice of schools imposed certain limitations on the applicability of our findings, some of which will be discussed in more detail later on (see pp. 154–7). It is, however, necessary to bear con-

[1] See pp. 199–208.

stantly in mind that these three schools were by no means representative of the whole field of secondary education, since two of them were selective schools and in the case of the comprehensive school our sample was taken only from the top six streams. Nor can we claim that they are necessarily typical even of schools of this kind. The comprehensive school for example was at the time of the study quite rigidly streamed, was predominantly working-class in its intake and had few children of above average ability.

Another limitation on the representativeness of our findings derives from the methods of sampling and analysis used in the study. Although we used several different kinds of sample, some of which permitted us to generalize, the main thrust of the analysis, particularly of the parental data, was concentrated on the 'extreme' groups of successful and unsuccessful boys. Although as a method this had the advantage of enabling us to focus our attention and our resources on relatively small and, from our point of view, highly significant groups, the fact that these groups were not randomly selected means that we cannot legitimately generalize our findings. Consequently the conclusions we draw must be regarded as exploratory rather than definitive, and we would repeat that our intention has been to explore the possibilities of adopting a new approach to the study of school achievement which would pave the way for other researchers to follow, rather than to establish specific relationships or confirm or refute hypotheses. It is in this somewhat tentative spirit that we offer these findings.

CHAPTER TWO

PROFILES OF SUCCESS
AND FAILURE

I DIMENSIONS OF PERSONALITY

In outlining the plan of this study it has been shown that we depended largely upon two sources of data: the boys themselves and their parents. Moreover, although the parental interviews took up a great deal of our resources and gained only limited data, the boys, thanks to the co-operation of the schools, provided us with a very fruitful avenue of information which could be obtained with relative ease, since they were both a captive and a willing group. For this reason we are able to present a fairly detailed picture of the kind of boy who was successful and the kind of boy who was unsuccessful in the three schools in the study. Moreover, because we were able to use questionnaires administered to a whole class, most of the information about the boys is available not just for the extreme groups, or even for a random sample, but for the main sample consisting of all the boys starting school in a particular year or (in the case of the comprehensive school) in the academic block of six streams. In the main, however, such data will be referred to only if the extreme group analyses show a significant relationship with success.

There is, however, another reason for beginning the account of our findings with the boys themselves. A number of studies of

the factors involved in differences in school achievement set out
to examine the relative importance of the pupils' environment.
For example, they may attempt to assess the significance of the
home versus the school or, within the home, of material factors
versus parental attitudes. In fact, however, in so far as school or
home backgrounds influence school achievement they do so not
directly, but by means of their influence on the child. Consequently it makes sense to examine the successful or unsuccessful
pupils as a first step in an analysis which leads from the child to
his achievement whether in the home or in the school. Some
selectivity was necessary and we focused on the major statistically derived dimensions of personality extraversion and neuroticism, dependence and conformity, and achievement orientation.

2 EXTRAVERSION AND NEUROTICISM

There is now fairly general agreement among experimental
psychologists about the two major dimensions of personality:
neuroticism and extraversion. The former dimension is frequently regarded as a reflection of the ease with which a
person's anxiety is aroused while the latter tends to be associated
with an outgoing, social and impulsive style of life.

Much work has been done relating these traits to school
achievement,[1] but findings have tended to be inconsistent and
the correlations have not usually been high. Such findings have
stemmed from a proliferation of simple correlational studies,
and it is clear that what are necessary are more sophisticated
research designs which give due regard to factors which have
been suggested as contributory to the complex patterns of
results. These include the age of the subjects, their ability, their
study habits, the methods of teaching used and the possible
interaction effects between the two traits themselves or between
either of them and other characteristics such as interest and
achievement motivation. Thus, for example, when considering

[1] H. J. Eysenck, 'Personality and attainment: an application of psychological principles to educational objectives', *Higher Education*, I (1)
(1972), pp. 39–52.

the possible relationship that anxiety might have with success, it may be that it differed according to whether one was considering extraverts or introverts. In this study regard was paid to age, factors associated with the schools and the possible interaction between anxiety and extraversion.

To measure these variables, all the pupils in the main sample, i.e. all the boys included in the study, were given the Junior Eysenck Personality Inventory[1] at the beginning of their second year. Examples of items from each of the two scales are given below:

Extraversion
   (a) Can you get a party going?
   (b) Do you like mixing with other children?
Neuroticism
   (a) Do you ever feel 'just miserable' for no good reason?
   (b) Does your mind often wander off when you're doing a job?

In order to pay regard to age, school climate and possible interaction effects the methods used to analyse the results in relation to the two personality traits were more intensive than with other personality and motivational factors. In addition to the cumulative measure of success based on progress over the first three years, the achievements of the boys were studied longitudinally making use of the main sample. The 11-plus scores were examined together with the achievement scores[2] which the boys obtained from the school examinations at the end of the first, second and third years, when they were approximately 12, 13 and 14 years old. Within each school, on the basis of the boys' scores on the Junior Eysenck Personality Inventory, four groups were formed, viz., extraverts who scored high on neuroticism, extraverts who scored low on neuroticism, introverts who scored high on neuroticism and introverts who scored low on neuroticism, and the achievements of these groups

[1] S. B. G. Eysenck, 'A new scale for personality measurement in children', *British Journal of Educational Psychology*, XXXV (3) (1965), pp. 362–7.
[2] For the method of calculating these scores see appendix 2, p. 198.

were subjected to analysis of variance. The numbers in each of the groups within each school were equalized by random selection.

Within any school the ability of each personality group as measured by the 11-plus verbal reasoning test was similar, and hence any subsequent differences in achievement between the groups cannot be attributed to that factor.

As regards the English and arithmetic tests of the 11-plus,[1] the extraversion/introversion dimension was not related to performance in any of the school groups. This was also true of neuroticism, with the single exception of the arithmetic test where, in one of the three schools only, the high neuroticism group scored higher than the low neuroticism group ($F = 5.663$, $p < 0.5$).

In the school examinations, however, introversion was significantly related to academic achievement in both the traditional grammar and the technical grammar schools. In the traditional grammar school there was indeed a consistent trend for all introvert groups to do progressively better over the three years, and there is thus some support for the view that introversion becomes more important with older children. In the comprehensive school on the other hand no consistent trend of any kind was noted in the school performance of extravert and introvert groups. While the different findings for the various school groups might be due to chance as a result of the small numbers of children in each of the groups it is possible that level of ability influences the effect of introversion/extraversion, since ability, as measured by the 11-plus, was highest at the traditional grammar schools, where the relationship was most marked, and lowest at the comprehensive school where no relationship existed. On the other hand the explanation may lie just as plausibly in differences between the schools. At the traditional grammar school, for example, achievement expectations were high and demands were made in both home and school for sustained periods of study. Homework loads were higher than at

[1] See appendix 4, Tables A2. 1–10, pp. 209–13 for the tables on introversion/extraversion and neuroticism.

either of the other schools, and there was less emphasis on non-academic subjects such as games, art and music. Such a school environment may well prove more congenial to the introvert, since it has been found that they tend to be more persistent students than extraverts, and more accurate and reliable. They are also said to be more interested in books than people. These points will be taken up again later, in a comparison of the three schools as different contexts of learning.

In the case of neuroticism, an even more complex pattern of relationships emerged, both between schools and over time. In the comprehensive school, the school attainments of each of the high neuroticism groups tended to be higher than those of the stable groups. In the grammar technical school high neuroticism also tended to favour achievement until the third year, when for all those within the introvert group neuroticism became a disadvantage. In the traditional grammar school neuroticism was a disadvantage for the introvert group from the first year and for the extraverts from the second year. Only in the third year in the last school was the difference significant. It is tempting to explain these differences also in terms of the differing levels of academic pressure and expectation for achievement in the three schools. High internal drive would be an advantage in relation to academic achievement, where external pressures or expectations for achievement were low. This could explain the advantage of high neuroticism in the comprehensive and grammar technical schools where school and parental pressures were lower than in the grammar school. In this school, where external pressures were greatest, high internal drive is mainly a disadvantage to pupils.

None of the interaction effects in any of the schools or years was significant, but there were interesting changes in the relative performance of the two high neuroticism groups in the grammar and grammar technical schools. In the former school, at the age of eleven, the extraverted group are marginally better than their introvert equivalents. In the first year of the secondary school the difference has swung marginally in favour of the introverted group. In the second and third years this tendency for the neurotic introverts to improve with age and for the neurotic extraverts to deteriorate steadily increases.[1] In the grammar technical school, on the other hand, the tendency is for neurotic introverts relatively to deteriorate in the second and third years.

Apart from examining the relationships over time between personality and achievement using the main sample, we also looked at the same relationships for the extreme groups of successful and unsuccessful pupils, i.e. those who were extreme over- and under-achievers after three years, in terms of their performance in the 11-plus.[2] Making use once more of an analysis of variance design, the differences between the extreme groups in neuroticism scores were found to be very small, but there was a significant relationship between success and introversion ($F = 8.88$, $p = < .01$).[3] The pattern was the same in each of the schools, including the comprehensive school, suggesting the possibility that the introversion/extraversion dimension may be a factor in extreme success or failure, as we have defined it, even when, as in the data from the main sample for the comprehensive school, it does not appear to be related to achievement in general.

3 DEPENDENCE AND CONFORMITY

The third major aspect of personality to be taken into account by this study was the dependence/independence dimension. A number of researchers in the United States have shown that at the college level independence is related to academic performance,[4] although at the high school level there is some evidence that the dependent pupils achieved better.[5] Strodtbeck

[1] D. S. Finlayson, 'A follow-up study of school achievement in relation to personality', *British Journal of Educational Psychology*, XL (3) (1970).
[2] For an account of the selection of these groups see appendix 2, pp. 196–8.
[3] For the relevant tables see appendix 4, Table A2.9, p. 213.
[4] D. E. Lavin, *The Prediction of Academic Performance* (New York, Russell Sage Foundation, 1965).
[5] H. Gough, 'What determines the academic achievement of high school students', *Journal of Education Research*, XLVI (1953), pp. 321–31.

26 *Success and Failure in the Secondary School*

has also suggested that independence from the family and other social groups is related to achievement.[1] It seemed therefore important to include some measure of this personality dimension in the analysis.

It was decided to use a test designed by Flanders[2] for his studies of classroom interaction, in which he defines a dependent pupil as one who is primarily concerned with pleasing the teacher. 'As he works on a problem, he is more concerned with what the teacher wants than he is with whether or not his method will solve the problem.' Items referring to conformity to parents' wishes and conformity to peer group wishes were compounded, together with some general items dealing with a preference for dealing with difficulties without reference to others, on the assumption that dependence, and its associated susceptibility to social influence, were unitary concepts. It was decided to make use of Flanders' test, but to distinguish items referring to dependence on parents from those referring to peers.

Out of a total of forty-five items, some of which were modified to suit the English context, thirty-two were retained, following item analysis.[3] The items had, as their themes, positive and negative instances either of seeking help, approval and affection or of conformity and compliance. Examples of the items include:

(a) I do not like to ask for help from others
(b) I enjoy reading about things my parents don't like
(c) I never break the gang rules.

The dependent-proneness scores of the extreme groups of successful and unsuccessful boys, based on the third year

[1] F. L. Strodtbeck, 'Family integration, values and achievement', in A. H. Halsey, J. Floud, and C. A. Anderson (eds.) *Education, Economy and Society* (Free Press, 1961), pp. 331–2.
[2] N. Flanders, 'Some relationships among teachers' influence, pupil attitudes and achievement', in B. J. Biddle, and W. J. Ellena (eds.), *Contemporary Research on Teacher Effectiveness* (New York, Holt, Rinehart and Winston, 1964).
[3] The split-half reliability, corrected by the Spearman-Brown formula, derived from fifty random scripts was 0·672. The normally distributed scores had a mean of 18·68 and a standard deviation of 4·36.

cumulative scores, were compared using analysis of variance. The differences between the groups were not significant[1] although the mean score of the successful group in every school was higher—indicating greater independence – than that of the corresponding unsuccessful group ($F = 2 \cdot 28$). These differences were most noticeable in the grammar and grammar technical schools. In order to derive a measure which distinguished between expressed conformity to adult wishes, as distinct from peer group pressures, the third year extreme groups' responses to those items dealing with adults on the one hand, and peers on the other, were scored separately.[2] The patterns of results obtained from the adult items was similar to that obtained from the use of the whole test but the relationship with success was now sufficiently marked to be significant ($p = < 0 \cdot 5$). In the comprehensive school, however, there were no differences in the scores of successful and unsuccessful boys on the adult items so that the relationship holds only for the two grammar schools. The effect of dependence on school achievement thus appears to depend on the degree to which achievement is valued by parents and other significant adults. Any detailed discussion of the meaning of these relationships must therefore be examined at a later stage in the analysis, but it is possible that the difference between the comprehensive school and other schools is related to a difference in parental values.

Taking the peer group items alone, the differences between the groups were small and no consistent pattern emerged. There was no evidence that dependence on peers was related, that is to say, either to success *or* failure. Again, however, it would seem that we must take into account not simply susceptibility to group pressure but also the nature of the pressure, if we are to give meaning to these findings.

A number of items in the interviews of the parents of the extreme groups also provided us with a possible behavioural measure of dependency or conformity on the part of the boys. These items, although derived from the parents, all describe the

---

[1] For a fuller account of the analysis of these data see appendix 4, Table A2.11, p. 214.
[2] For details see appendix 4, Table A2.12, pp. 214–15.

boys' reaction to particular rules. Four of these items were concerned with homework, one with parental rules about friends,
and one with parental rules about hair. These items were used in
the interviews of the parents of the first year extreme successful
and unsuccessful groups, i.e. those based on the examinations at
the end of the first year, and the third year extreme groups, i.e.
those based on the cumulative performance over three years.
The replies of the parents were coded, and the coded items
related to success or failure, using χ^2. When these items were
related to success, unsuccessful boys were found to be less co-
operative than successful boys over parental rules about friends
in the case of both first year extreme groups (p = < ·01) and
third year extreme groups (p = < ·05). Unsuccessful boys were
also significantly less co-operative about hair rules in the first
year extreme groups (p = < ·01) and in the third year extreme
groups (p = < ·05).[1]

The relationship with success was less marked for the third
year extreme groups, since the number of unco-operative boys in
the unsuccessful group was much reduced. In the case of rules
about friends, for example, the percentage of cooperative boys
in the successful group rose from 66 per cent in the first year
extreme group to 79 per cent in the third year extreme group,
possibly reflecting a more permissive attitude on the part of the
parents to boys who were now two years older. In the case of unsuccessful boys, however, the increase was from only 18 per cent
in the case of the first year extreme group to 55 per cent in the
third year extreme group. We have reason to suppose that some
at least of these parents had become resigned to the disobedience
of their sons and relaxed their rules accordingly, a point which
will be taken up in more detail at a later stage (see p. 83).
It does however suggest a much more complex relationship
between child personality and parental behaviour than the
simple cause and effect model sometimes proposed.

The rest of the items were all concerned with homework.[2]
The parents were asked whether it was any trouble to get the
boy to do his homework and the replies were coded in terms of

[1] For details see appendix 4, Tables A2.13–19, pp. 215–18.
[2] For details see appendix 3, p. 204.

the boy's apparent acceptance or rejection of homework and homework rules. Perhaps not surprisingly, unsuccessful boys were less accepting of homework than successful boys, particularly in the case of the third year extreme groups (p < ·01). Successful boys, again according to their parents' reports, spent longer on their homework than unsuccessful boys. This was equally true in the case of both the first year and third year extreme groups (p= < ·01). The number of boys spending less than three-quarters of an hour a night on their homework did not change very much, but almost all of them, and in the case of the third year extreme groups all of them were unsuccessful boys. The third year extreme groups of parents only were also asked two further questions on homework, viz., whether the boys were now spending more or less time than before, and whether they were now taking more or less trouble than before. Successful boys were almost always taking more time and trouble than before, where unsuccessful boys were either spending the same amount of time and trouble or even less (p = < ·01).

The four items on homework were found to be related to each other and were scored to form a 'homework orientation' cluster.[1] When this homework orientation cluster for the third year extreme groups was related to success, using analysis of variance, a highly significant relationship was found (p = < ·01). Moreover, there was a trend for boys to be more homework-oriented as one moved from the comprehensive through the grammar technical to the grammar school. This exactly parallels the importance attached to homework by the school as judged by the amount of it which is given.

This last measure can be regarded as a reflection of the academic mores of the schools. When it is taken together with the earlier finding that successful boys in the third year were taking an increasing amount of time over their homework while unsuccessful boys took the same or less time, the findings are consistent with Eysenck's theory about extraversion which in an earlier section of this chapter was related to lack of success. He maintains that introverts will become conditioned more easily

[1] For details of this procedure see pp. 199–201.

than extraverts to the academic mores which make for success and that long-continued application to study will set up inhibition more easily in extraverts than introverts with the former consequently engaging in avoidance tendencies.

These statistical relationships are illustrated well in the following two case studies of a successful and an unsuccessful boy taken from the interviews with grammar school parents.

In the case of Malcolm Green, a highly successful boy, his parents described him as 'never a naughty child', and a boy who 'gets upset if he upsets anybody'. As parents the Greens exert firm but by no means rigid control over Malcolm and reported very little in the way of problems. He 'never' answers back, although he will sometimes argue, which they did not count as answering back. He always gets on with his homework when he gets back from school, and is never any trouble about staying out late. If they think he is watching too much TV they suggest he does something else, although he never lets it interfere with his homework. He is a boy who worries about things and sometimes needs assurance over his school work. When asked if there was anything they would like to change about him, both parents agreed that he was a 'bit on the shy side' but they 'would not like his character to alter'.

Norman Smith is a complete contrast. His parents had been told at the primary school that he was a very clever boy, but even then, according to their account, it was always a problem to make him work and attend to lessons. Encouraged by the headmaster, however, they chose the traditional grammar school, and were delighted when he was given a place and put in one of the top forms. Even in the first year, however, he had difficulty in getting down to work and after the first year examinations he was placed in one of the lower forms. The parents were very disappointed, especially as this meant that he had to drop Latin. According to their account he was not really poor at any of the main subjects, and school work was no effort 'when he gets down to it'. The parents described him as a sociable boy who 'must be popular', but who was also easily led. His many activities and interests included Scouts and he was particularly keen on camping.

Two years later the Smiths, interviewed a second time by a different interviewer, reported that Norman, now fourteen, never does any homework, at least not at home. On the odd occasion when he brings something home the work has taken about ten minutes. They had also given up bothering him about it, since he only gets upset when they mention it. By this time, too, discipline seems to have broken down altogether. Norman was reported to be going out every night with his friends in spite of his parents' wish that he would stay in more. Yet they do not make any demands because 'he would get very sulky'. It was the impression of both interviewers that the Smiths had very little control over their son. This is not to suggest that every success-ful boy was like Malcolm Green or every unsuccessful boy was like Norman Smith, and certainly some successful boys needed more pressure than Malcolm while some unsuccessful boys were trying hard. Nevertheless, by the time of the fourth year inter-view, nineteen of the unsuccessful boys were a problem over their homework compared with only nine of the successful boys. Similarly only ten of the unsuccessful boys were no problem over homework, compared with twenty of the successful boys. At this time, when homework demands were heavy in all schools, all the successful boys were spending more than three-quarters of an hour a night on their homework, but only thirteen of the twenty-nine unsuccessful boys.

4 ACADEMIC ORIENTATION

Homework orientation was initially regarded as an index of dependence on adults, particularly parents. It has, however, been shown to be consistent with personality theory relating to introversion. It may also be seen, in part at least, as arising out of the boy's own liking for intellectual pursuits. Kahl, in a study of twelve high achieving and twelve low achieving boys of similar ability and socio-economic status in the United States, found no cases in which school work gave sufficient intellectual satisfaction to supply its own motivation. None of the boys, he writes, 'was interested in learning for the subtle pleasures it can

offer, none craved intellectual understanding for its own sake'.[1]
While Kahl is therefore inclined to dismiss the idea of intellectual curiosity providing its own motivation for working hard, it
does not follow that this might not be an important factor in the
different setting of the British school system, and in selective
schools. Moreover, the small scale of Kahl's study makes it
unwise to generalize from his findings even within American
society.

Consequently a scale of intellectual curiosity was devised.
Examples[2] of items include:

(a) working out answers to complicated problems whether
    they seem useful or not
(b) thinking about what life on other planets may be like
(c) finding out the meanings of odd words.

When the intellectual curiosity scores of the third year extreme
groups were analysed, successful boys were seen to have markedly higher scores, and analysis of variance produced a highly
significant F ratio.[3] This relationship was not sustained when
the analysis was extended to the whole year group,[4] though in
each school, the unsuccessful boys had markedly lower scores
than the other groups. There were no differences between
schools. One might have expected that boys in the traditional
grammar school, because of their previous high achievement as
reflected in their 11-plus results, would have gained higher
scores than the rest. In fact, the school mean for the traditional
grammar school was 7·44, for the technical grammar school
8·0 and for the comprehensive school 7·57.

A more direct approach was also used to discover whether

---

[1] J. Kahl, 'Common man boys' in A. H. Halsey, J. Floud, and C. A.
Anderson (eds.) *Education, Economy and Society* (Free Press, 1961,
p. 357).
[2] Some of the items were borrowed from Stern's Pupils' Activities
Index, and a number of others were constructed for this scale. After
item analysis, sixteen items remained which had an estimated reliability according to the Kuder-Richardson formula of .782.
[3] For further details see appendix 4, Table A2.20, p. 218.
[4] For further details see appendix 4, Table A2.21, p. 219.

successful boys had more intellectual interests. All the boys, during their second year at school, were asked a number of questions about the kind of activities they were involved in outside school, and the responses to these questions were categorized and coded. When these responses were related to achievement it was found that only in the traditional grammar school were intellectual hobbies and interests significantly related to success, although a very slight trend in this direction was noted in the other two schools. Successful boys in all the schools preferred spending time alone, although this trend also was more marked at the traditional grammar school.

A further questionnaire asked about friendship choices. Of these, friendship with girls proved to be the most interesting for our purpose. There were three items, whether a girl was listed among their three best friends, whether they liked to spend time with girls and whether they actually did spend time with girls. The responses to these three items were combined to form an 'interest in girls' cluster score.[1] When the third year extreme groups were compared, using analysis of variance, successful boys were found to be less interested in girls than unsuccessful boys in each of the three schools, although the difference is very slight in the comprehensive school. Overall however the difference between successful and unsuccessful groups is significant ($F = 13 \cdot 03$, $p = < \cdot 001$)[2] although this is largely due to the quite large differences between the successful and unsuccessful groups in the two grammar schools. Although successful boys in all three schools showed a similar attitude towards girls, the unsuccessful boys in the comprehensive school showed less interest than did successful boys in the other two schools. The fact that the comprehensive school was coeducational, whereas the two others were single-sex schools, may however be the reason for the different pattern of results.

At the time this questionnaire was given the boys were only 12–13 years old, and we are not implying any lasting relationship

[1] All of these items were found to be significantly related to each other, with one exception in the comprehensive school. For further details see appendix 3, pp. 207–8.
[2] See appendix 4, Table A2.22, p. 219.

between academic success and lack of interest in girls. But the early interest in girls taken by unsuccessful boys in the two single-sex schools seems again consistent with their tendencies to extraversion, their liking to be with others rather than be alone and their preference for sport and social activities rather than intellectual hobbies.

5 ACHIEVEMENT ORIENTATION

Orientations refer to the different ways in which individuals view their world and themselves in relation to it. As Rosen put it, 'they act as spectacles through which the individual sees himself and his environment'.[1] Florence Kluckhohn[2] has represented the orientation of the dominant American culture as emphasizing man's relation to nature as one of mastery, the response to time as future-oriented, activity as doing rather than being, i.e. active rather than passive, and relationships as individualistic rather than familial or collectivistic. The combination of these orientations is hypothesized as orientating an individual towards achievement.

Several studies have examined the relationship between these *achievement* orientations and school achievement with conflicting findings. Rosen, for example, found that a scale which compounded three orientations – active/passive, present/future and familialistic/individualistic – was related to the educational aspirations of high school boys but *not* to their actual achievement as measured by school grades. Strodtbeck,[3] also using compounded scores, found that a group of over-achieving boys had higher scores than a group of under-achieving boys. Sugarman,[4] in a British study, found no consistent relationship across

[1] B. C. Rosen, 'The achievement syndrome: a psychocultural dimension of social stratification', *American Sociological Review*, XXI (1956) pp. 203–11.
[2] For a general critique see J. A. Kahl, 'Some measurements of achievement motivation', *American Journal of Sociology*, LXX (1965), pp. 669–81.
[3] F. L. Strodtbeck, op. cit.
[4] B. Sugarman, 'Social class and values related to achievement and conduct in school', *Sociological Review*, XIV (1966), pp. 287–301.

schools. In an endeavour to clarify the relationship of these orientations to achievement in this study the scores were not compounded but aspects of achievement orientations were considered separately.

The individualistic/familialistic orientation was derived from the hypothesized necessity of the achieving individual to relinquish group ties, especially if they are a handicap to him in the achievement process. It was decided therefore that the measure of dependent proneness could be regarded as a suitable measure of this particular orientation. As has been shown, independence was associated with lack of success rather than success. Furthermore, it will be shown that successful boys had particularly warm and close relationships with their parents. It may be that this finding is a result of the age of the boys in this study, and that as adolescence proceeds, relationships within the family will change. As however there is no evidence to suggest that this is likely to happen, and as independent measures from both boys and parents were in the same direction, it was not considered necessary to make any further endeavour to examine this orientation.

The active/passive orientation is concerned with power over the environment; an active orientation is one which implies a belief that mastery over one's fate is possible. Passively orientated individuals, by contrast, tend to believe that the world is unpredictable, determined by fate or by powerful groups or individuals. Although this conception has been used very widely to explain differences in achievement between individuals, and between social groupings such as socio-economic and racial or ethnic categories, there is no generally agreed way in which such an orientation can be measured.[1] After a comprehensive review of both the sociological and psychological literature in this field it was decided to make use of the Children's Intellectual Achievement Responsibility Questionnaire devised by Crandall in studies of school achievement in the United States.[2] The

[1] See especially J. A. Kahl (1965), op. cit.,
[2] V. C. Crandall, W. Katkovsky and V. J. Crandall, 'Children's beliefs in their own control of reinforcement in intellectual-academic achievement behaviour', *Child Development*, XXXV (1965), pp. 91–109.

merit of this particular measure from our point of view was the concrete nature of the items, which appeared to relate to the child's own experience and were expressed in personal terms. As the name of the questionnaire implies, it is intended to measure not general ideas about luck or fate, but the extent to which children actually attribute responsibility for events to themselves or to others, i.e. the extent to which they see themselves as masters of their own fate.[1]

The format of Crandall's questionnaire was followed and some of the original items were used, but a number of additional items were added in order to make the instrument more suitable for the age group of the boys in our study.[2] Examples of items are given below:

1 Suppose you have something you wanted very much. Would it probably be
  (a) because you are usually lucky anyway?
  (b) because you had done a great deal of work?
2 If you failed to get an important job would it probably be because
  (a) you did not know the right people?
  (b) you did not know the answers to some of the questions in the interview?
3 If you found that you were just not quite good enough to get into one of the school teams in your favourite sport, would you
  (a) train and practise at the sport until you were good enough to get into the team?
  (b) just accept the fact that you were not good enough?

Boys were asked to choose between the two alternatives according to the way of looking at the situation they thought they would adopt. They were then scored in terms of their belief in

[1] For a general discussion of beliefs at the level of the individual subject see D. S. Finlayson, 'Towards a psycho-sociological view of school achievement', *British Journal of Educational Studies* xxi (2) (1973).
[2] Following item analysis, a final twenty-two items were retained, whose reliability according to the Kuder-Richardson formula was .645. The distribution of scores was normal.

an internal or external locus of control over events, i.e. whether they had an active or passive orientation. This questionnaire was given to all the boys.

When the three schools were compared using analysis of variance, it was found that there were significant differences between schools, with the mean score highest for the traditional grammar school and lowest for the comprehensive school.[1] Within schools however, there was no consistent pattern of relationship between scores and success or failure when the third year extreme groups were compared. In the comprehensive school, scores were not related to success; in the traditional grammar school, the successful boys tended to believe in an external locus of control, and in the technical grammar school in an internal locus of control.[2] There is therefore no simple relationship between this particular orientation and achievement. It may be that it operates in interaction with other variables producing a highly complex rather than a straightforward patterning within schools.

The future/present orientation refers to the time span within which events are considered. It is possible, on the one hand, to lay out plans for the future and seek to relate present actions and achievements to these explicit goals. On the other hand it is possible to live in the present without considering the possible relationship of present events to the intentions, which themselves may or may not be expressed. This involves both the ability to articulate relationships between what is going on in the present and what may occur in the future in order to relate present activities to future goals, and the ability to delay immediate gratification for the sake of future reward. Kahl's attempt to categorize families in terms of 'getting ahead' or 'getting by' is perhaps one of the best-known studies which has attempted to relate present/future orientation to school achievement. He found that his low achieving boys shared a family outlook which emphasized just 'getting by', and looked 'neither to the past nor the future'. Boys who believed in 'getting ahead' were 'prepared to sacrifice

[1] See appendix 4, Table A2.23, p. 220.
[2] See appendix 4, Table A2.24, p. 220.

adolescent freedom and fun in order to channel more energy into school work'.[1]

The willingness to defer gratification in this way will of course depend upon the value placed upon the future goal, and possibly too upon the level of confidence that the goal will be achieved. It must be supposed, too, that boys with an academic orientation who enjoy their school work will not face the same necessity to reconcile future satisfaction and present needs, since they will be in accord.

In order to measure future/present orientation a further questionnaire was constructed which sought to assess the extent to which the pupils valued the future and the changes associated with it. Examples of the items included in the final version are given below.[2]

1 If you are offered a part-time job, is it better to
   (a) turn it down in case it interferes with your school work?
   (b) take it, for you will have money in your pocket to spend?
2 When you are young, is it better to
   (a) enjoy yourself while you can?
   (b) do things that will help you later on, even if you don't like doing them now?

As with the active/passive orientation measure, there were significant differences between schools when school means were compared, using analysis of variance[3] with the most future-oriented boys at the traditional grammar school, and the least at the comprehensive school. Within schools, however, no consistent pattern between successful and unsuccessful boys emerged when the third year extreme groups were compared, although there were tendencies in this direction in both the traditional grammar school and the comprehensive school for the more future-oriented boy to be more likely to be successful.

[1] J. A. Kahl, (1961) op. cit., pp. 354–9.
[2] It was difficult to find items which discriminated within our sample, and the reason may be associated with the normative nature of many of the items. Only twelve items were retained after item analysis. The estimate of reliability of the test, using the Kuder-Richardson method, was ·559 which is rather lower than is desirable.
[3] See appendix 4, Table A2.25, p. 220.

In the grammar technical school, however, the mean score of the two groups, although very close together, was in the opposite direction.[1] Again, therefore, this particular variable does not appear to have any simple relationship with school achievement.

The significant and consistent differences which were found between the schools for the active/passive and future/present orientation do however require explanation. One possibility suggested by the different levels of ability in the three schools is that boys of high ability are more likely to express active rather than passive and future rather than present orientations, but when the two orientation measures were correlated with the 11-plus verbal reasoning scores, no such relationship was found. Indeed the coefficients in each case were of a zero order. The second possibility is that the pupils were expressing the expected beliefs prevalent in each of the schools rather than their personal values. This would certainly be in line with what we know of the different atmosphere and traditions of the three schools. It is also noteworthy that the measure of dependent proneness is significantly correlated ($p = < \cdot01$) with both the active/passive and the future/present orientations ($r = \cdot291$ and $\cdot279$), since dependent boys are more likely to express conventional beliefs and values. Such an interpretation suggests the possibility that forced-choice questionnaires may encourage conventional responses rather than the personal beliefs of individual pupils, an issue which will be raised in more detail in the following chapters.

6 CONCLUSION

This review of certain of the personality characteristics, interests and value orientations of the successful and unsuccessful boys is derived mainly from the analyses of differences between the extreme groups. It provides us with a preliminary but logically consistent picture of the kind of boy likely to be successful in the schools we studied and possibly, although we cannot be sure of this, in other similar schools as well. He will, more likely than

[1] See appendix 4, Table A2.26, p. 221.

not, be an introvert, have a dependent relationship with his parents, be conformist or compliant rather than rebellious, be intellectually curious, willing to apply himself to homework, to enjoy his own company and to have, at least in single-sex schools, little interest in girls. Given the tradition of our selective schools, with their emphasis on hard work, on academic standards and the ability to work unsupervised at home, none of this is particularly surprising. Such a boy will be more likely than other boys to accept discipline and particularly perhaps the self-discipline involved in success in such an environment, partly because of his more compliant nature, but partly also because his academic interests are likely to make school work more congenial to him. The complex pattern of results which emerges within schools in relation to the active/passive and future/present orientation suggests that further consideration should be given to the problem of measurement. When that is done, a further examination of the relationships may be worthwhile within particular school contexts .

One of the most obvious aspects of personality associated with success or failure either at school or in later life, the presence or absence of the motivation to succeed, has not so far been considered. This factor has been examined in many ways, under different labels. Turner, for example, has studied it under the heading of ambition, and McClelland has looked at it more narrowly, but in greater depth, in terms of what he calls need for achievement or achievement motivation. The next chapter deals with our findings in this particular area.

CHAPTER THREE

THE WILL TO SUCCEED

1 WHAT IS ACHIEVEMENT MOTIVATION?

The motivation or will to succeed may, at the commonsense level, appear to be an important element in achievement whether at school or elsewhere. Yet understanding of the part it plays in school achievement is severely handicapped by the difficulty of definition and of measurement in this particular area. Motivation is normally seen as an inner drive or compulsion, the true nature or strength of which may not be apparent at the conscious level, so that it cannot be tapped by the simple process of question and answer. The attempt to measure motivation by means of questionnaire items, or even by an interview, also faces the problem of conventional rather than 'true' responses, particularly in a society like our own, which has a high regard for achievement and for ambition. The use of occupational and educational aspirations as a measure of the motivation to succeed is also open to a number of serious objections. Turner,[1] for example, has pointed out the importance of relative rather than absolute measures of ambition. He makes use of what he calls the ladder rather than the race model of mobility, arguing that some start higher up the ladder than others, rather than all

[1] R. Turner, *The Social Context of Ambition* (San Francisco, Chandler, 1964).

starting at the same point, as in a race. Consequently it may take as much ambition for an unskilled labourer to move into the skilled labour category as for a small business owner to move into a managerial position in a large business. His own study showed that although boys of higher social background had higher aspirations, they were in fact less ambitious in relative terms if ambition is measured by the number of jumps they hoped to move up the occupational ladder. If Turner is right, therefore, it is only safe to compare educational and occupational aspirations at the same socio-economic level, if they are intended to serve as indications of motivation to succeed.

Other lines of criticism have focused on the difference between aspirations and expectations. Some authors have denied that the working classes value success any less than the middle classes, and claim that the difference lies chiefly in the expectation of achieving it. Stephenson,[1] for example, claimed that in both Britain and the USA the working-class student was more likely to have expectations lower than aspirations. More significantly, expectations of success may actually influence aspirations, so that low expectations depress aspirational level. Support for some sort of interaction between the two is provided by Caro and Pihlblad[2] who found the greatest disparity between aspirations and expectations among low achievers. If this view is the correct one, the correlation between aspiration and achievement, which has been frequently noted, reflects a much more complicated relationship than is usually supposed, and it is as reasonable to consider high aspirations the effect of school success as it is to conceive of them as a cause.

One way of evading some complexities of the value/aspiration/expectation problem is to use a projective measure of motivation instead of one which relies on direct formulation as in questionnaires and interviews. One of the most common projective measures is that designed by McClelland. In this the subject is presented with a set of pictures and asked to make up a story

[1] R. M. Stephenson, 'Stratification, education and occupational orientation', *British Journal of Sociology*, IX (1958).
[2] F. G. Caro and C. T. Pihlblad, 'Aspiration and expectations', *Sociology and Social Research* XLIX (1965), pp. 465–75.

about them. These stories are then scored for evidence of achievement motivation using an elaborate scoring system devised and developed by McClelland and his associates.[1] It is assumed that the frequency of imagery involving striving for success and fear of failure is a valid indicator of an internal drive for achievement. This inner drive is to be distinguished from the value expressly placed on achievement by the subject.

Projective and questionnaire measures of achievement motivation are frequently unrelated to each other[2] and this lends support to the view that they are tapping different aspects of personality. De Charms,[3] after reviewing relationships between both kinds of measures and other variables concluded that scores on questionnaires may tend to reflect the expectations that significant others have for a subject's performance, and that projective measures are a better indication of internalized motivational tendencies.

It was felt necessary, therefore, to include both types of measure in our study, and to examine their relationship not only to school success and failure but also to each other. Similarly, measures of educational and occupational aspirations and expectations were collected from both the boys and their parents. In order to throw some light on the relationship between aspirations, expectations and achievement, a small follow-up study was mounted in one of the schools, and some longitudinal material was collected from parents. Although the small numbers involved make it difficult to be positive about findings, it is hoped that they are adequate to throw some doubt on the conventional way of interpreting the relationship between aspirations and achievement.

[1] D. C. McClelland, *The Achievement Motive* (New York, Appleton, 1953).
[2] D. C. McClelland, 'Risk-taking in children with high and low need for achievement', in J. W. Atkinson (ed.) *Motives in Phantasy, Action and Society* (Princeton NJ, Van Nostrand, 1958).
[3] R. De Charms, *et al* 'Behavioural correlates of directly and indirectly measured achievement motivation' in D. C. McClelland (ed.) *Studies in Motivation* (New York, Appleton, 1955).

2 PROJECTIVE AND QUESTIONNAIRE MEASURES OF ACHIEVEMENT MOTIVATION

The rationale behind the projective measure, as has already been indicated, is that achievement imagery reflects achievement drive or need for achievement as McClelland calls it. This refers to a need, believed by McClelland to be learned, to perform tasks in a manner which reflects high standards of excellence. For the purposes of our study four pictures were selected,[1] each considered suitable for eliciting achievement motivation imagery, and slides of these were projected to the boys in their classrooms. The pictures, in the order shown, were as follows:

(a) boy seated at a desk with an open book in front of him
(b) two inventors working on a machine
(c) man seated at a drawing board
(d) boy with vague operation scene in the background.

Following each projection of a slide, four minutes were allowed for the boys to write a story in which they were asked to indicate

What is happening now?
What has led up to this situation?
What are the people thinking?
What will happen?

Although the test was given to all the boys, time only allowed the stories of the successful and unsuccessful groups to be scored for achievement motivation. The skewed distribution of scores was now dichotomized into high and low groups and the difference between the successful and unsuccessful groups was tested for significance by χ^2. This was done within each school and overall. Table 3.1 shows the number of boys with high 'need for achievement' scores and low need for achievement scores in each of the successful and unsuccessful groups.

[1] The help of W. P. Robinson in connection with the selection of the slides and with the scoring method is gratefully acknowledged.

Table 3.1 *A comparison of need for achievement scores between successful and unsuccessful boys*

	(n = 70) Grammar		(n = 50) Grammar technical		(n = 45) Comprehensive		(n = 165) Combined	
	High n/ach	Low n/ach	High n/ach	Low n/ach	High n/ach	Low n/ach	High n/ach	Low n/ach
Successful	19	11	16	9	11	10	46	30
Unsuccessful	16	24	9	16	10	14	35	54
χ^2 value	3·73		3·92		0·52		7·37	

Although in only one school, the grammar technical, does the value of χ^2 reach the level of significance ($p = < ·05$), in the traditional grammar school it just falls short of significance. A similar but much less noticeable trend is found in the comprehensive school. When all the schools are combined successful boys are found to have significantly higher ($p = < ·01$) need for achievement scores than unsuccessful boys. The consistency of these findings is interesting in view of the inconsistency of earlier attempts to substantiate a link between need for achievement and actual achievement.[1] It has been suggested by way of comment on the inconsistency that, in certain situations, the achievement motive may not be aroused, and this may be a consideration in the comprehensive school where the relationship is so slight. While this 'lack of arousal' explanation might still be tenable in the day-to-day school work situation, it does not stand up in the achievement motivation testing situation for, when compared two at a time, no differences were found between schools in the levels of achievement motive of the combined successful and unsuccessful groups.

A number of non-projective measures of achievement motivation were also devised. The first of these was a questionnaire which attempted to assess by direct questions the extent to which a pupil derived satisfaction from striving and exerting personal effort. This will be referred to as the scale of *expressed*

[1] E. Klinger, 'Fantasy need achievement as a motivational construct', *Psychological Bulletin*, LXVI (1966), pp. 291–308.

achievement motivation since it is intended to tap the same needs or drives as McClelland's projective test. Examples of the items[1] include

(a) driving myself to see how much I can do
(b) doing something difficult just to prove I can do it
(c) giving up on a problem rather than doing it in a way that might be wrong
(d) setting higher standards for myself than anybody else would.

When the scores of the successful and unsuccessful extreme groups were compared, using analysis of variance, there was a tendency for successful boys to have significantly higher expressed achievement scores ($F = 15 \cdot 18$, $p = < \cdot 001$).[2] As was the case with need for achievement, the comprehensive school showed a much smaller difference than the other two schools.

The scores of all the boys in all three schools were also compared. The differences between the schools were in an unexpected direction, since the mean scores were highest at the comprehensive school and lowest at the traditional grammar school. Since the differences between schools were very small and not statistically significant little attention need be paid to them.

Apart from the scale of expressed achievement motivation the attempt was made to construct a scale of phantasy achievement.[3] Examples of the items are

(a) thinking about what I could do that would make me famous
(b) pretending I am a great movie star.

This particular scale, however, showed no relationship with success or failure. Nor were there any significant differences between schools. This suggests that preferences for achievement

[1] Following item analysis eighteen items were retained. The scores were randomly distributed and the reliability coefficient, estimated by the Kuder-Richardson formula, was ·693.

[2] See appendix 4, Table A3.1, p. 221.

[3] The split-half reliability estimated by the Kuder-Richardson formula was ·815 and the scores were normally distributed.

in phantasy situations or daydreams could be regarded as reflections of a personality characteristic that does not appear to influence or be influenced by real experiences of achievement.

In order to examine this hypothesis and to throw some light on the complexity of relationships associated with the questionnaire measure of expressed achievement, a three-by-three analysis of variance design was used.[1] Neuroticism, need for achievement and school success were the independent variables. The first two of these variables have been conceptualized as motivational drives and the last measure will have associated with it feedback experience of achievement in school with ability controlled. For the design, eight groups were assembled, four of successful boys and four of unsuccessful boys. Under each of these categories were four groups made up of different combinations of drive or motivational conditions – high neuroticism/ high need for achievement, high neuroticism/low need for achievement, low neuroticism/high need for achievement, low neuroticism/low need for achievement.

When the expressed motivation scores are examined for each of these groups, the lack of relationship between expressed motivation and need for achievement, as measured by projective techniques, is confirmed for our study. If, however, success and failure in school is introduced as a moderating variable, a pattern of relationships becomes clear. Boys with high need for achievement who are *successful* at school also have high expressed motivation, while those who are unsuccessful have low *expressed* motivation. The same can be said of boys who have high neuroticism scores. The converse is the case with boys low in achievement motivation and neuroticism.

These findings suggest that unsuccessful boys responded to their lack of success according to their level of motivation as measured by the need for achievement score, and their drive as measured by the neuroticism score. Boys who were highly moti-

[1] A full account of this analysis is described in D. S. Finlayson, 'Expressed achievement motivation in relation to the achievement motive, neuroticism and school success', *British Journal of Educational Psychology*, XLII (1) (1972), pp. 65–70. See also appendix 4, Tables A3.2–3, p. 222.

vated and with high drive or neuroticism scores denied their motivation when asked to express their motivation for success, a response which could well be interpreted as a rationalization of their failure. Unsuccessful boys with low motivation and low drive, by contrast, tended to express unrealistically high levels of striving, perhaps to convince others and perhaps themselves that they were really trying, when they were not. Such an interpretation is highly speculative but it does explain the pattern of our findings, and those of others. Sears for example has remarked on the unrealistic level of aspiration of unsuccessful children[1] and much of the work associated with Atkinson's theory of motivation[2] is consistent with it.

If this interpretation is correct it suggests that questionnaire measures of expressed motivation cannot be regarded as simple measures of motivation. Nor as De Charms suggests do they merely reflect the expectations of significant others. Rather they are associated with a highly complex interactional pattern involving motivation levels, drives, the expectations of others and the experience of success or failure. To what extent they are causal to or consequent upon achievement is an open question.

When a similar analysis was done with phantasy achievement as the dependent variable it proved to be related only to neuroticism. This confirmed the hypothesis formulated earlier that phantasy achievement was associated with a personality characteristic, not experience of actual achievement.

3 PUPIL ASPIRATIONS AND EXPECTATIONS

Aspirations, as has already been suggested, cannot be used as simple indices of motivation, particularly if Turner's ladder model of social mobility is accepted as more appropriate than the model of a race. On the other hand, aspirations may be seen more legitimately as indicating the value placed on different

[1] Pauline S. Sears, 'Levels of aspiration in academically successful and unsuccessful children', *Journal of Abnormal and Social Psychology*, XXXV (1940), pp. 498–536.
[2] J. W. Atkinson and N. T. Feather, *A Theory of Achievement Motivation* (New York, Wiley, 1966).

education and occupational levels and the acceptance of these values as goals towards which it is necessary or desirable to strive. Consequently, questionnaire items were included in the study to tap both educational and vocational aspirations.

Two measures of educational aspiration were included, one relating to the school and the other to higher education. The school aspirations were expressed in terms of the certificates of external examining boards and school leaving age, and responses were coded into four categories, below O level GCE, O level, A level and beyond A level. The pupils were also asked their expectations of achieving these goals so that the relationship between aspirations and expectations could be compared.

Table 3.2 gives the aspirations and expectations, expressed as percentages, of the boys in the main sample, i.e. all the boys in the study, collected during their second year at school.

Table 3.2 *Level of pupil educational aspirations and expectations, expressed as percentages*

School	Level							
	Below GCE		O level GCE		A level GCE		A level +	
	Asp.	Exp.	Asp.	Exp.	Asp.	Exp.	Asp.	Exp.
Traditional grammar	3	1	7	26	34	40	56	33
Grammar technical	4	1	24	38	36	41	36	20
Comprehensive	23	17	23	37	24	29	30	17
Combined	8 (n = 24)	4 (n = 15)	15 (n = 49)	32 (n = 100)	32 (n = 102)	38 (n = 119)	45 (n = 142)	26 (n = 82)

It will be seen that all the aspirations are high, since only 8 per cent of the boys do not aspire to GCE although the percentage of boys in this category is considerably higher at the comprehensive school. Even at the comprehensive school, however, as many as 54 per cent aspired to A levels or above which, given the borderline nature of the ability of entrants, is very high indeed. It should be noticed, too, that in 1964 there were only 12 A level passes at the comprehensive school as compared with 37 at the grammar technical school and 293 at the traditional grammar school. On the other hand, and in spite of the high aspirations at the comprehensive school, the level of aspiration at the traditional grammar school is significantly higher than in either of the other two schools (p = < ·001). Aspirations are also higher at the grammar technical school than at the comprehensive school (p = < ·05).

The level of expectations can also be seen to be generally high, since 64 per cent of the boys expect to obtain at least an A level qualification. This is so even for 36 per cent of boys at the comprehensive school. Both expectations and aspirations were in fact unrealistically high at this stage. However, they still reflect differences between the schools in the actual number of A level passes achieved, since expectations were highest at the traditional grammar school and lowest at the comprehensive school, (p = < ·001).

When we consider aspirations in relation to expectations there is a fairly sharp drop in level, supporting previous findings in this area. Thus although 77 per cent aspire to reach A level, only 66 per cent expect to do so. This represents forty-three boys who expect to have to leave after O level when they would like to stay on for A level or beyond. In the case of boys with low aspirations there are few who do not expect to reach them and, in the case of boys whose aspirations are below O level GCE, expectations are higher than aspirations. Probably these were boys who wanted to leave school as quickly as possible but knew that they would be expected to try for O level as a result of pressure from either parents or school. Such boys are however very few in number in comparison with those who expect to succeed at a lower level than their aspirations.

The aspirations of the main sample for higher education are shown in Table 3.3. It can be seen that these were also high. Only 4 per cent of the sample had no aspirations for further education, and in each school far more boys wished for full-time than part-time higher education. Overall, almost half of the boys wanted to go to a university. The aspirations of the traditional grammar school pupils are significantly higher than those

Table 3.3 *Level of pupil higher education aspirations expressed as percentages*

School	Level			
	None	Part-time	Full-time	
			Tech/ College	University
Traditional grammar	4	12	21	63
Grammer technical	1	27	31	41
Comprehensive	7	35	26	32
Combined	4 (n = 13)	22 (n = 68)	25 (n = 77)	49 (n = 155)

in the other two schools (p = < ·01). Though the technical grammar school boys have higher aspirations than the comprehensive school boys the difference is not significant.

Vocational aspirations were also high, and 52 per cent of the main sample chose a professional career of some kind. The pupils in the traditional grammar school were the most likely to have professional aspirations (68 per cent) and the comprehensive school pupils the least likely (30 per cent), with the grammar technical school pupils in an intermediate position (40 per cent). The difference between the traditional grammar and the other two schools is significant (p = < ·01).

When the two main measures of educational aspiration are examined in terms of school achievement as measured by cumulative performance over three years, high aspirations are related to success, although this tendency is not significant in the grammar technical school. Pupil expectations are also related to school achievement, although only in the case of the comprehensive school is this tendency significant (p = < ·05). Vocational aspirations are significantly related to success in the comprehensive school (p = < ·05), where the spread of aspirations is greatest, but not in the traditional grammar school where more than three-quarters of the boys had professional aspirations.

In general, therefore, both aspirations and expectations appear to be related to school achievement, although there are differences between schools. The most consistent pattern occurs with respect to the comprehensive school, possibly because there is the greatest spread of aspiration and expectation in this school.

To test this relationship in another way, the four items were now interrelated, using χ^2, and were found to form a related cluster.[1] The items on vocational aspirations were however dropped from the analysis at this point because of their limited spread and differences in distribution between the schools. The other three items were combined into what we have termed an educational goal and achievement cluster.[2] When the resultant scores are compared for the third year extreme groups, using analysis of variance, there is a relationship between high educational goal achievement and success ($p = < \cdot 01$).[3] This is in line with a very considerable body of research relating aspirations to achievement.

4 PARENTAL ASPIRATIONS AND EXPECTATIONS

In the many attempts to relate school achievement to family background the place of parental aspirations has played a dominant part. A large number of studies have shown that parental aspirations for their children are related to school achievement.[4] Such findings have most frequently been explained in terms of behaviour and attitudes arising out of these aspirations, and which are held to be conducive to successful school performances. For example, such parents encourage their children to read books, to try hard at school and to do their homework conscientiously. They may also influence their

[1] The tables of χ^2 value are shown in appendix 3, pp. 202-3.
[2] For the method of scoring see appendix 3, p. 204.
[3] For further details see appendix 4, Table A3.4, pp. 222-3.
[4] O. Banks, *The Sociology of Education* (2nd edition, London, Batsford, 1971), chapter 4.

children more directly by teaching them to value school achievement and occupational success, and this may be internalized by the children as a need for achievement, or achievement motivation.

Because of the importance placed on parental aspirations in previous studies of school achievement, it has inevitably played a large part in our own inquiry. An attempt to estimate the general level of aspirations of the parents was made by means of the interview of a random sample of parents during the boys' first year at school. In the course of this interview, both mothers and fathers were asked their preferred school leaving age. They were also asked to name a preferred career but such a large number refused to commit themselves on this that no further use was made of this question. Table 3.4 gives the preferred age of leaving school for both parents in each school separately, expressed as a percentage.

Table 3.4 *Parents' preferred school leaving age : random sample expressed as percentages*

Preferred age of leaving school	Mothers			Fathers		
	Tradi-tional grammar	Grammar tech-nical	Compre-hensive	Tradi-tional grammar	Grammar tech-nical	Compre-hensive
18 or above	93·2	86·0	73·7	97·5	92·3	70·3
Below 18	6·8	14·0	26·3	2·5	7·7	29·7
Total	100·0	100·0	100·0	100·0	100·0	100·0
	n = 44	n = 43	n = 38	n = 40	n = 39	n = 37

Aspirations were highest for parents with sons at the grammar school, but even at the comprehensive school where aspirations were lowest a sizeable majority of parents wanted their sons to stay on until eighteen or over. The difference between the grammar school and the comprehensive school, but not between the other schools, was significant ($p = < ·01$).[1]

Further analysis, however, shows that the figures for the comprehensive school conceal an important difference within the school itself. The academic block at the comprehensive school

[1] χ^2 was used throughout this analysis.

was at this time made up both of boys who had 'passed' the 11-plus and a nearly equal number of boys who had 'failed' but who were selected for inclusion in the academic block on the basis of an internal examination given by the school itself at the start of their school career. For purposes of convenience these two groups will be known as selective and non-selective pupils, although no distinction was made by the school itself and members of staff were unaware into which group any pupil fell. These two groups varied little in ability or in socio-economic background. A comparison of the parental aspirations showed, however, that the aspirations of the parents, and particularly the mothers, of selective boys were markedly higher. Of the mothers of selective boys, twenty preferred a leaving age of eighteen or above and only one a leaving age below eighteen. In the case of the non-selective boys, eight mothers chose eighteen or more, and nine below eighteen. This difference is significant ($p = < \cdot01$). In the case of the fathers the differences are similar but slightly less pronounced ($p = < \cdot05$).

These findings are of course in line with other research which has demonstrated the relationship between 11-plus success and parental aspirations. The meaning of this relationship has however still to be examined and will be discussed later. What does merit comment at this stage is the similarity of the replies of the parents of selective boys in all three schools in spite of the differences in the reputations of the schools and the abilities of the pupils. As will be shown later there were also considerable differences between the schools in the socio-economic status of the parents.

In order to examine the relationship between aspirations and school achievement, a number of questions were included in the interviews of the parents of the extreme successful and unsuccessful groups. The replies to these questions were coded and the two extreme groups compared, using χ^2. Table 3.5 gives the replies of fathers to a question on the preferred leaving age, coded into two categories, eighteen years and above, or below eighteen.[1] The replies of parents of both first year and third

[1] The replies of the mothers were very similar and have not therefore been included.

Table 3.5 *Fathers' level of educational aspiration : first and third
year extreme groups*

Extreme group	Successful		Unsuccessful	
	18+	*18—*	*18+*	*18—*
1st year	31	1	16	12
3rd year	22	4	13	10

year extreme groups are included. Although there are significant differences between the parents of successful and unsuccessful boys (p = < ·05), the most striking thing to be noticed
about Table 3.5 is the high parental aspirations even of the
fathers of unsuccessful boys.

Parents were also asked at what age they expected their sons
to leave school, and the replies of the fathers to this question are
given in Table 3.6. Fathers of unsuccessful boys had signi-

Table 3.6 *Fathers' level of educational expectation : first and third
year extreme groups*

Extreme group	Successful		Unsuccessful	
	18+	*18—*	*18+*	*18—*
1st year	29	2	9	18
3rd year	23	4	12	13

ficantly lower educational expectations for their sons (p = < ·01)
Indeed, the difference between successful and unsuccessful
groups is greater for expectations than for aspirations. The
expectations of fathers of successful boys are in fact no lower
than their aspirations, whereas although 56·5 per cent of the
fathers of unsuccessful boys in the third year extreme group
aspired to a school leaving age of eighteen plus, only 48·0 per
cent expected their sons to achieve it.

A final question on further education also revealed a very high
level of parental aspirations, since the great majority of parents

c

expressed a wish for some form of further education or training. In order to discriminate between the replies, they have been coded into university education and other forms of higher education. The replies of fathers are given in Table 3.7. The

Table 3.7 *Fathers' higher educational aspiration: first and third year extreme groups*

Extreme group	Successful		Unsuccessful	
	University	Non-university	University	Non-university
1st year	20	11	10	15
3rd year	22	6	9	16

tendency for fathers of successful boys to have higher aspirations is again apparent and is particularly marked for the third year extreme group ($p = < \cdot 01$).

As a further check on these findings the responses of mothers and fathers were combined into a score on each of these three items,[1] and the third year extreme groups compared, using analysis of variance. When this is done, there is a consistent and significant tendency for parents of successful boys to have higher aspirations than the parents of unsuccessful boys, confirming our previous analysis, using χ^2 ($F = 10 \cdot 06$, $9 \cdot 763$, $p = < \cdot 01$). The differences between the schools were not significant, although the traditional grammar school parents, as in the random sample, tend to have higher aspirations than parents in the other schools. Nevertheless the direction of the relationship is perfectly consistent.

The educational expectations of parents of successful boys are also consistently higher than those of parents of unsuccessful boys[2] ($F = 12 \cdot 56$, $p = < \cdot 001$). The differences between schools are now significant ($F = 3 \cdot 62$, $p = < \cdot 05$), the expectations of parents steadily increasing from the comprehensive school through the technical grammar to the traditional

[1] For further details see appendix 4, Tables A3.5–6, p. 223.
[2] For further details see appendix 4, Table A3.7, p. 224.

grammar school. The parents of successful boys do not however contribute to this trend, and their expectations are in fact fairly similar in all schools. It is the parents of unsuccessful boys whose expectations drop increasingly from the traditional grammar to the comprehensive school.

5 ASPIRATIONS, EXPECTATIONS AND ACHIEVEMENT

So far in this chapter we have examined the relationship of aspirations and expectations to achievement for both parents and boys with very consistent findings. Expectations have also been shown to be markedly lower than aspirations in the case of unsuccessful, although not successful, boys. It seems reasonable to suppose, therefore, that the level of expectation is influenced by the level of achievement, and that changes in achievement of a dramatic kind can have a significant impact on the educational expectations of both parents and pupils. In this sense, expectations are seen as a consequence rather than a cause of school achievement. For this to be the case, however, it must be demonstrated that not only the boys but also their parents were aware of the 'under' and 'over' achievement of the particular pupils falling into our extreme groups. To test this the parents were asked to assess, on a five-point scale, their son's ability in relation to other boys of his own age, and also their perception of how well he was doing at school. Mothers' and fathers' responses were collected separately but were found to be very similar and were combined into a single parental score. The third year extreme groups were then compared using analysis of variance.[1] There was a consistent and significant tendency for parents of successful boys to have a higher opinion of their son's ability in comparison with other boys ($F = 16.69$, $p = < .001$) and to perceive him to be doing well, or very well, at school ($F = 23.61$, $p = < .001$). The relationship between the parents' perception of the boys' progress and our measure of achievement was in fact very close, as only three out of twenty-five parents of successful boys said their son was not doing well or very well. Similarly out of twenty-four unsuccessful boys, only

[1] For further details see appendix 4, Tables A3.8–9, pp. 224-5.

five parents said their son was doing well or very well. Clearly, therefore, these parents were interested enough in their son's progress to have perceived the deterioration or improvement which had resulted in their selection by us as extremely successful or unsuccessful boys, and which would have been conveyed to them in school reports, in promotion or demotion between or within forms and in some cases in problems over homework.

It is not surprising, therefore, to find that parents with educational expectations *lower* than their educational aspirations making comments like 'we don't think he'll make it' when questioned about the discrepancy in their responses. In these cases, clearly, the interviews showed that the educational expectations were a response to the parents' perception of the boy's poor performance at school.

In fact, however, as the earlier tables show, there were not many parents with such a discrepancy between aspirations and expectations and most parents in fact gave the same reply to both questions. The point that arises, consequently, is the extent to which both aspirations and expectations are influenced by the parents' knowledge of their son's progress at school. This is a more novel approach, since aspirations are more usually taken as a measure of the extent to which parents value education or are ambitious for the children's educational or occupational success. In fact, however, there is already a certain amount of evidence that parental aspirations are influenced by school achievement. Barker Lunn[1] for example has produced evidence of both upward and downward changes in parental aspirations as a result of streaming.

So far as this study is concerned, it has already been suggested that success in the 11-plus may have acted to raise parents' aspirations, and that allocation to the academic block in the comprehensive school may have had the same effect, but this is largely supposition on our part, since the data are very meagre. Of greater weight are the parents' own comments, made during

[1] J. C. Barker Lunn, *Streaming in the Primary School* (Slough, NFER, 1970). See also D. S. Finlayson, 'Parental aspirations and the educational achievement of children', *Educational Research* XIV (1) (1971), pp. 61–4.

the course of the interviews of the extreme groups, in answer to the question on higher educational aspirations. Once parents had made their choice they were encouraged to give the reason for their particular answer. Thus pressed, many parents replied wholly or sometimes partly in terms of their son's ability or progress. Surprisingly enough, this type of response was characteristic not only of parents of unsuccessful boys, but also of parents of successful boys with high aspirations. Phrases like 'we think he has the ability to get ahead' and 'we would not want to waste his ability' are typical. Implied in such answers, although not always openly expressed, is a belief in the benefit of a university for those able to profit from it. Parents of unsuccessful boys shared this belief in the value of a university education but did not think it a *realistic* aspiration for their son. Thus the father of one unsuccessful boy at the traditional grammar school chose teacher training because this didn't need so many A levels, adding 'I think university may be a little too high to aim for.' Other parents, too, justified their choice of teacher training in this way, with the phrase 'we don't think he'll make university.' The choice of full-time or part-time technical education was sometimes made in terms of the boy's practical interests, e.g. 'he likes using his hands', coupled with his dislike of school. The parents of one boy (at the comprehensive school) with unusually low aspirations – they wanted him to leave as soon as possible – saw him as having wasted his school years. With no prospects of doing any good at school, 'he might as well leave.'

In making these judgements, therefore, the parents were expressing not only their perception of the relative value of different types of higher education but also its relevance for their own child. A university, in this context, is for the clever boy and the hardworking boy, but for the boy who is doing badly at school, and particularly the boy who is perceived by his parents as not trying at school, it is no longer a meaningful or realistic aspiration. Not all the parents of unsuccessful boys lowered their aspirations in this way; as we can see from Table 3.7, nine out of a total of twenty-five fathers of unsuccessful boys still aspired to a university education for them. In some cases the parents did not seem to be fully aware of the situation at school or its implications; in other cases they expressed their aspirations in a conditional way by saying 'if he manages to get A level'. Parents of boys in the traditional grammar were particularly likely to retain high aspirations in spite of their son's lack of success at school, perhaps because, as we have seen, success at A level was much more likely at this school and may not therefore have been seen as so conditional on a high level of school achievement.

On the whole, therefore, parents seemed to be strongly aware of the value of educational qualifications and were often bitterly disappointed at what they perceived as a failure on the part of their sons to take advantage of an opportunity they had themselves been denied. As one mother of an unsuccessful boy at the traditional grammar school put it, 'I tell him he'll never get on, and end up with a job like his dad's, on the road all hours.' This boy's father was a long-distance lorry driver, and her reaction is by no means untypical. Many mothers saw educational qualifications as a means of escape from the long hours worked by their husbands in sometimes very arduous working conditions.

These comments suggest that parental aspirations are the product of a highly dynamic process in which the feedback of information about the pupil's progress at school plays an important part. Further evidence which supports this point of view is provided by answers given by the random sample of parents during the boys' first year at school. These parents were asked what, in their view, a parent should do when faced with the two following hypothetical questions:

(a) a boy is doing very well at school but wants to leave as soon as he reaches the school leaving age at fifteen
(b) a boy is not doing very well at school and wants to leave as soon as he reaches the school leaving age at fifteen.

Table 3.8 summarizes the responses of the random sample of parents to these two questions. Because there was little difference between schools the responses from all three schools are combined. The difference in the pattern of response to these two situations is very considerable. Parents were much more likely to say 'let him leave' if he was not doing well at school,

and much less likely to refuse to let him leave or even try to persuade him to stay (p = < ·001). These declared intentions on
the part of the parents of this sample lends considerable support
to the view that parents react to information about a child's
progress at school and temper their expectations and aspirations
for their child in the light of that information.

Table 3.8 *Responses of parents to hypothetical situations on school
leaving age*

Parental response	Boy is doing well		Boy is not doing well	
	Mother	*Father*	*Mother*	*Father*
Refuse to let leave	34(27·0)	30(24·6)	2(1·6)	2(1·7)
Persuade to stay	70(55·6)	70(57·4)	11(8·7)	18(14·9)
Let leave	22(17·5)	22(18·0)	114(89·8)	101(83·5)
Total	126(100·0)	122(100·0)	127(100·0)	121(100·0)

At the same time they showed that they were well aware of
the importance of education in relation to vocational opportuni-
ties and that such utilitarian considerations underlay the high
aspirations they expressed. Their comments in the course of the
interview indicated that this willingness to keep a boy at school
was primarily a reflection of the value attached to a 'good job'
and the appreciation by these parents of the growing importance
of educational qualifications as a means of securing one. As one
parent with a son at the comprehensive school put it, 'you need
a ticket now to get anywhere'. Unless staying on at school was
going to lead to these qualifications it was, as some of the parents
of unsuccessful boys were to put it later, a waste of time.

6 A LONGITUDINAL STUDY

In order to examine the relationship between aspirations, expectations and achievement more precisely, a follow-up study was

undertaken of the boys in the grammar technical school. In common with all the boys in the study they had completed questionnaires giving details of both their educational aspirations and expectations, and these have been described in an earlier section of this chapter, along with the replies of the boys in the other two schools. At the end of their third year they were asked to complete a further questionnaire covering the same ground. While ideally all the schools should have been included in this second phase, time and resources did not allow this, and one school had to be selected. The grammar technical school seemed a particularly good choice because in this school streaming was introduced at the end of the second year. In the traditional grammar school this decision was taken largely at the end of the first year, and in the comprehensive school streaming was introduced from the start. In the technical grammar school, therefore, we would, by comparing the answers of the boys during their second year and their third year, be able to consider the effect of the introduction of streaming on aspirations and expectations.

Table 3.9 compares the second and third year aspirations and expectations of the boys involved. For the purpose of comparability only those boys are included for whom replies are available on both occasions.

Table 3.9 *Comparison of educational aspirations and expectations in the second and third year of technical grammar school boys*

Item	Category	2nd year	3rd year
Examination aspirations	O level	20	37
	A level	49	32
Examination expectations	O level	28	41
	A level	41	28

Aspirations drop quite markedly between the middle of the second year when the first questionnaire was given and the end of the third year when the questionnaire was repeated.

Table 3.10 repeats this information in terms of their achievement according to their cumulative achievement scores over the first three years.

Table 3.10 *Comparison of educational aspirations and expectations in the second and third year of technical grammar school boys by achievement*

Groups	2nd year				3rd year			
	Aspirations		Expectations		Aspirations		Expectations	
	O level	A level	O level	A level	O level	A level	O level	A level
Successful	2	19	6	15	4	17	7	14
Achieving as expected	10	21	14	17	17	14	19	12
Unsuccessful	8	9	8	9	15	2	15	2
χ^2	6·72		1·82		18·18		11·83	
Contingency coefficient	·298		·160		·457		·382	

In the second year, although there is a tendency for both aspirations and expectations to be related to success, only the relationship for aspirations is significant ($p = < ·05$). In the third year, both items are significantly related to success ($p = < ·01$) and the contingency coefficients show that in the third year the relationship is markedly greater. It will be noticed, however, that there has been little change in the aspirations and expectations of the successful group. What has happened is that the achieving as expected, and even more so, the unsuccessful groups have reduced both expectations *and* aspirations.

The higher education aspirations of the boys as a whole were slightly lower in the third year, when forty-one boys opted for full-time higher education as compared with fifty in the second year, although there was little sign of any change in vocational aspirations. When, however, we look at the responses of the boys in relation to their level of achievement, the picture is rather different.

Table 3.11 *Comparison of higher educational and vocational aspirations in the second and third year of technical grammar school boys by achievement*

Groups	2nd year responses			
	Higher educational aspirations		Vocational aspirations	
	Part-time	Full-time	Professional	Other
Successful	7	14	14	7
Achieving as expected	7	24	12	17
Unsuccessful	7	10	3	11
χ^2	1·91		7·27	
Contingency coefficient	·164		·319	
	3rd year responses			
Successful	3	18	16	4
Achieving as expected	14	17	0	24
Unsuccessful	12	5	1	10
χ^2	12·45		35·76	
Contingency coefficient	·391		·628	

Vocational aspirations are significantly related to success in both the second year ($p = < \cdot 05$) and third year ($p = < \cdot 01$) but a comparison of the two contingency coefficients shows the relationship to be very much more marked in the third year, by which time only one boy not in the successful group still retains aspirations for a professional career. In the case of higher education aspirations, again the contingency coefficients show a marked increase in the relationship. As in the previous items the change has again been in the unsuccessful and achieving as expected groups, whose aspirations have fallen markedly.

To test the hypothesis that changes in educational aspirations and expectations were related to streaming, such changes for pupils allocated to different forms were compared.[1] It was found that those pupils who had actually raised their level of aspirations and expectations were almost all from those who had been allocated to the upper form. A fall in aspirations or expectations was as we have seen more frequent, but was significantly more likely among pupils going into the lower stream ($p = < \cdot 01$ using the McNemar test). A similar but less marked pattern was found for higher education aspirations and vocational aspirations.[2]

The results of the longitudinal study, therefore, do a great deal to support our argument that both expectations *and* aspirations are affected by the actual experience of school success and failure. We have also tried to show in earlier sections that this appears to be the case for both parents and boys. Although we have not been able to do any detailed mapping out of the factors which act as information for either parents or pupils, we have suggested that the 11-plus and streaming may well act in this way and so may more subjective impressions. For example, parents often seemed to take their cue from their son's unwillingness to do homework and his general attitude to school and school work.

This way of looking at aspirations clearly has many implications and these will be explored in subsequent chapters. In the meantime we turn to look more closely at other aspects of the family background of successful and unsuccessful pupils. Only then will it be possible to relate the motivations and personality of the child to both achievement and family structure and family relationships.

[1] See appendix 4, Tables A3.10–11, pp. 225-6.
[2] See appendix 4, Tables A3.12–13, p. 226.

CHAPTER FOUR

PATTERNS OF CHILD-REARING

I PARENTAL BEHAVIOUR AND SCHOOL ACHIEVEMENT

The preceding chapters have made some attempt to describe the personality and motivation of the highly achieving child, but this is only a part of the question we set ourselves to answer. We must now go on to consider how far parental attitudes and behaviour, and family background, are related not simply to school achievement itself, but more importantly to those aspects of personality and motivation which make achievement possible. As a step in this direction we look first at previous work on patterns of child-rearing and the ways in which these have been related to a number of measures of achievement. From that work, two main aspects of child-rearing have been identified – the love/hostility and control/autonomy[1] dimensions.

In the first of these a number of studies have produced fairly consistent findings though involving different pupil and parental variables. Douvan,[2] for example, in a comparison of upward- and downward-aspiring high school boys relative to

[1] E. S. Schaefer, 'A circumplex model for maternal behaviour', *Journal of Abnormal and Social Psychology*, LIX (1959), pp. 226–35.
[2] F. Douvan and J. Adelson, 'The psychodynamics of social mobility in adolescent boys', *Journal of Abnormal and Social Psychology*, LVI (1958), pp. 31–44.

their fathers' occupations, and using the boys' perceptions of their parents, found that upward-aspiring boys were more likely to report a congenial relationship with their parents. Another study, using much younger children, by Katkovsky[1] found that children of parents rated by interviewers as protective, nur-turant, approving and non-rejecting were more likely to believe that they had mastery over their environment. A study of over- and under-achievers, homogeneous in intelligence and socio-economic status, also found that over-achievers were more likely to describe their families as affectionate.[2] Similarly, Milner[3] emphasized the factor of emotional warmth in a study of reading ability in grade one school children.

On the issue of control versus autonomy, Becker[4] has recently summarized a large number of studies which show that children exposed to restrictive discipline are more conforming and more dependent than children exposed to more permissive disciplinary techniques. An experimental study by Rosen and d'Andrade[5] found that fathers of boys who were high scorers on projective measures of achievement motivation often appeared to be competent men who were willing to take a back seat while their sons were performing, although the mothers became emotionally involved in the boy's success. They suggested that dominating fathers seemed to be a threat to the boys. A similar

[1] W. Katkovsky, V. C. Crandall and S. Good, 'Parental antecedents of children's beliefs in internal-external control of reinforcements in intellectual achievement situations', *Child Development*, XXXVIII (1967), pp. 765–76.
[2] W. R. Morrow and R. C. Wilson, 'Family relationships of bright high achieving and under-achieving high-school boys', *Child Development*, XXXII (1961), pp. 501–9.
[3] E. Milner, 'A study of the relationships between reading readiness in Grade 1 school children and patterns of parent/child interaction', *Child Development*, XXII (1951).
[4] W. C. Becker, 'Consequences of different kinds of parental disci-pline', in *Review of Child Development Research*, I (1964) (eds. M. Hoffman and L. W. Hoffman, Russell Sage Foundation), pp. 169–208.
[5] B. C. Rosen and R. d'Andrade, 'The psychosocial origins of achieve-ment motivation', *Sociometry*, XXII (1959), pp. 183–218.

point has been made by Strodtbeck[1] in relation to measures of achievement orientation. A cross-national survey[2] found a relationship between reports of authoritarian parental relationships and low educational achievement in the United States, in Great Britain and in East Germany, even when social class was controlled. This finding is confirmed by Morrow and Wilson[3] who, in their study of over-achieving and under-achieving high school boys, found that over-achievers were more likely to describe their families as relatively non-restrictive. Somewhat different results, however, were reached by Drews and Teahan[4] who, in a study of mothers of over- and under-achievers matched for socio-economic status and of high and average intelligence, found that it was the mothers of the over-achievers who were more authoritarian. Milner[5] too in the study already cited found that parents of high scorers in reading used more controls and prohibition.

All of these studies imply a linear relationship between parental authority and achievement; that is to say, that the more or less authoritarian the parent the greater or less the level of achievement. Bronfenbrenner,[6] however, has argued that the effect of parental discipline may be curvilinear, so that both too much *and* too little discipline may have similar effects. In a study of adolescents he found that high levels of responsibility as rated by teachers were associated with reports by the boys and girls of moderately strong discipline, and that both lack of discipline and strong discipline, especially from the father, were associated

[1] F. Strodtbeck, 'Family integration, values and achievement' in D. C. McClelland (ed.) *Talent and Society* (Princeton, NJ, van Nostrand, 1958).
[2] G. H. Elder, Jnr., 'Family structure and educational attainment, a cross national analysis', *American Sociological Review*, XXX (1965), pp. 81–96.
[3] W. R. Morrow and R. C. Wilson, op. cit.
[4] E. M. Drews and J. F. Teahan, 'Parental attitudes and academic achievement', *Journal of Clinical Psychology*, XIII (1957), pp. 328–32.
[5] E. Milner, op. cit.
[6] W. Bronfenbrenner, 'Some familiar antecedents of responsibility leadership in adolescents', in L. Petrullo and B. M. Bass (eds.), *Leadership and Interpersonal Behaviour* (New York, Holt, 1961).

with low levels of responsibility. Baumrind[1] also makes the point that to think in terms of authoritarian or permissive discipline is not sufficient. She proposes a third type of discipline, authoritative. In this type of discipline, the parents attempt to direct the child's activities in a rational, issue-oriented way. Reason is used to justify parental demands, and where children refuse to conform, objections are solicited. Both autonomous self-will and disciplined conformity are valued by an authoritative parent. Firm control is exercised at points of child/parent divergence, yet the child is not hemmed in with restrictions. His individual interests and special ways are recognized, yet standards are set for his future conduct. McClelland[2] seems to be making a similar point when he argues that indulgent parents who make too few demands of the child, and parents who make demands which are too early or too excessive, are both likely to produce children with low achievement motivation.

Another area of research in child-rearing is concerned with the various methods of rewarding and punishing which parents employ with their children. A number of studies[3] have been carried out to determine which methods seem to be the most effective in securing conformity from the children to parental expectations and, although these studies use different measures, there is a common core of agreement that the use of approval or disapproval as disciplinary techniques, and the use of reasoning and explanation, are conducive to the development of conscience. The use of coercive methods of discipline, on the other hand, including the use of physical punishment, appear to result in a moral orientation based on the fear of authority. The explanation which is advanced for the effectiveness of love-oriented methods of handling children is that children internalize parental expectations as a means of retaining parental warmth

[1] D. Baumrind, 'Effects of authoritative parental control on child behaviour', *Child Development*, XXXVIII (1967), pp. 888–907.

[2] D. C. McClelland, *The Achieving Society* (Princeton, NJ, van Nostrand, 1961).

[3] See for example H. Bandura and R. H. Walters, *Adolescent Aggression* (New York, Ronald Press, 1959) and R. Sears, E. Maccoby and H. Levin, *Patterns of Child Rearing* (Evanston, Row and Peterson, 1957).

and protection. Consequently, the internalization process tends to be most successful in a family environment where there is frequent and warm interaction between parent and child, but where training and discipline evoke a fear of the loss of love.

The use by parents of love-oriented techniques of discipline, and reasoning rather than physical punishment, appear to be related to pupils' achievement motivation. Rosen and d'Andrade[1] have observed, for example, that mothers of high school boys rewarded a good performance with warmth and approval and a poor performance with disapproval. Douvan[2] found an association between upward-aspiring boys and their perception of their parents as using verbal rather than physical methods of discipline, and Elder,[3] also using boys' perception of their parents, found the boys' aspirations related to the use of parental explanation. Using a rather different approach, Rosen[4] attempted to measure the extent to which mothers and their sons actually shared the same values. Mothers whose sons had similar values were more likely to report the use of affection, reasoning and appeals to standards, rather than physical punishment.

Parents may also be considered as presenting models to their children, either perceptual or symbolic, of desired behaviour, but the process of learning associated with these models would appear to be highly complex.[5]

2 THE MEASUREMENT OF CHILD-REARING

Before going on to describe some of our own findings, it is necessary to say something of the methods by means of which

[1] B. C. Rosen and R. d'Andrade, op. cit.
[2] F. Douvan and J. Adelson, op. cit.
[3] G. H. Elder, Jnr., 'Parental power legitimation and its effect on the adolescent', *Sociometry*, XXVI (1963), pp. 50–65.
[4] B. C. Rosen, 'Family structure and value transmission', *Merrill-Palmer Quarterly*, X (1964), pp. 59–76.
[5] M. Argyle and P. Robinson, 'Two origins of achievement motivation', *British Journal of Social and Clinical Psychology*, I (1962), pp. 107–20.

data on child-rearing are obtained. Yarrow[1] has drawn attention to the discrepancy between the level of sophistication of theory and of methods of research in this field. Evidence is frequently obtained by interviews with mothers, often involving retrospective data, and actual observational studies, either in the laboratory setting or in the home, are rare. Yet mothers, as Yarrow points out, are extremely ego-involved reporters, and their responses cannot be taken at face value. Moreover, studies which have actually compared interview and observation measures of parent/child interaction tend to show low correlations,[2] although there appears to be less distortion with respect to recent events. Other studies have made use of children's perception of parental behaviour, but a comparison of reports from parents and children suggests a high level of inconsistency.[3]

On the other hand, observational techniques have their own problems, and in the presence of an observer parents are likely to strive to make a 'good' impression. There are also limitations on the range of parental behaviour that can be observed by this method. For certain kinds of data, therefore, the interview may be a more useful tool than observation. A further difficulty arises out of the high cost of observation. It takes a long time to observe even a few cases over a wide range of behaviour and this can only be carried out effectively by trained and experienced staff. Consequently we felt ourselves unable to make use of this particular method, and relied instead mainly upon interviews for our data on child-rearing patterns. These interviews were, however, long ones, and loosely structured, so that the interviewer and the parents were able to talk together freely. Three interviewers were involved, all female, and all having some previous experience. The opportunity was also taken, wherever possible, to observe the behaviour of the parents to each other, and,

[1] M. R. Yarrow, 'Problems of method in parent-child research', *Child Development*, XXXIV (1963), pp. 215–26.
[2] E. Bing, 'Effect of child-rearing practices on development of differential cognitive abilities', *Child Development*, XXXIV (1963), pp. 631–48.
[3] M. L. Kohn and I. E. Carroll, 'Social class and allocation of parental responsibilities', *Sociometry*, XXIII (1960), pp. 372–92.

wherever possible, towards the children. The parents were also asked to complete some questionnaires, but on the whole these were not successful. Parents disliked them, and there were a large number of refusals.

In order to avoid some of the problems associated with interviewing in this area, the questions were designed to obtain information in as indirect a way as possible, and the emphasis was on getting the parents to describe their feelings and experiences. This was considered to be particularly important wherever defensive reactions and conventional responses appeared likely. A very small number of retrospective questions were included, but on the whole we avoided asking about the past as much as possible. Moreover, although for practical reasons mothers and fathers had to be interviewed together, care was taken to record their replies separately. At the same time, our questions often sparked off a quite spontaneous discussion between the parents, and this was also noted and used in the final coding. To avoid bias, interviewers were not told whether the boy was in a successful or unsuccessful group. Nevertheless, the problems of measurement in this area should be borne in mind in interpreting the findings to be described in later sections of this chapter.

3 THE LOVE/HOSTILITY DIMENSION

It was recognized that this area was a particularly difficult one to investigate, since any direct questioning of the parents would not only tend to encourage defensive reactions but might also arouse hostility to the research itself. Another and even more serious problem arises out of the difficulty of measuring and indeed even defining the aspects of behaviour to be included in such a dimension. In an attempt to meet these problems a number of questions were devised which seemed to cover the more important aspects of the love/hostility dimension as it has been used in the past, and included such areas as the demonstration of affection within the family, problems and difficulties and the way they were handled, and areas of pride and criticism. These questions, which are set out in full in appendix 5[1] were

[1] See appendix 5, pp. 244–6.

designed primarily to get the parents to talk rather than to provide us with answers on specific points, and in fact it was found that evidence on this dimension of parent/child relationship tended to arise at many points in the interview. Consequently, although these particular questions remained the focal point, the whole interview was used to provide us with a number of global ratings.

Three aspects of the love/hostility dimension were distinguished for the purpose of further analysis, determined partly by previous work in the field and partly by the data collected in the interviews. These were:

(a) the extent to which the parents showed affection openly towards the child, i.e. were demonstrative

(b) the extent to which the parents showed approval of and pride in the child

(c) and the extent to which the parents seemed to have a close relationship with the child as an individual and showed a sensitivity to his personal needs.

Both parents were rated separately on a three-point scale, by two coders independently. Cases of disagreement between the coders were re-examined and if disagreement persisted these cases were placed in the intermediate category.

Parents were rated as high in the demonstration of affection when there was considerable evidence in the interview of the frequent and overt expression of affection, such as kissing at night or in the morning, and cuddling when the boy was ill or unhappy. A low rating on the other hand was given when any such displays of affection were wholly or largely absent, either because the relationship was one of actual hostility or because the demonstration of affection was deliberately avoided. One father, for example, believed in being strict and aloof as a matter of principle, and the interviewer was told by the parents that they had deliberately discouraged any show of affection.

Table 4.1 gives the rating for the demonstration of affection by both mothers and fathers for both the first and third year extreme groups. For the purpose of this table all three schools have been combined. Only a very few mothers received a low

Table 4.1 *Parents' ratings for demonstration of affection : first and third year extreme groups*

Parent	Success category	1st year groups			3rd year groups		
		High rating	Intermediate rating	Low rating	High rating	Intermediate rating	Low rating
Mothers	S	16	16	1	12	15	2
	US	11	16	1	10	17	2
Fathers	S	7	25	1	8	17	4
	US	5	11	12	6	13	10

rating and these were found equally in the successful and unsuccessful groups. Mothers of successful boys were more likely to be rated as highly affectionate but the difference was very small, especially for the third year extreme group, and in neither case was it significant (using χ^2). In the case of fathers there was a better spread, and a number of fathers were rated as showing little affection: most of these fathers had sons in the unsuccessful category although the difference between the two extreme groups was significant only in the case of the first year (p = < ·01). This particular rating therefore did not show a very close relationship with success. This may have been because of the difficulty of assessing parental behaviour in this area on the basis of an interview.

Table 4.2 gives the ratings on parental approval and pride in the boy for both first year and third year extreme groups. Again the schools are combined. The ratings were based simply on the amount of pride parents expressed during the interview. When the groups are compared, using χ^2, there is a consistent tendency for parents of successful boys to express more pride and approval and less criticism than the parents of unsuccessful boys. This difference was significant (p = < ·01) in the case of both groups. The pattern of relationships shown here is indeed quite striking. By the fourth year, when the parents of the third

Table 4.2 *Parents' ratings for approval of boy: first and third year extreme groups*

Parent	Success category	1st year groups			3rd year groups		
		High rating	Intermediate rating	Low rating	High rating	Intermediate rating	Low rating
Mothers	S	12	21	0	17	11	1
	US	3	17	7	5	15	9
Fathers	S	12	21	0	17	9	3
	US	1	18	9	3	17	9

year extreme groups were interviewed, the majority of parents of successful boys have been placed in the highly approving category, and very few indeed have been placed in the category of disapproving or critical parents. Parents of unsuccessful boys are very rarely highly approving.

Another measure of parental approval was obtained from a questionnaire item which asked parents to assess their satisfaction with the boys' school progress on a five-point scale ranging from very satisfied to very unsatisfied. The responses of the parents were then grouped into satisfied and not satisfied. Table 4·3 gives the responses of both mothers and fathers for

Table 4.3 *Satisfaction with boys' school progress: first and third year extreme groups*

Parent	Success category	1st year group		3rd year group	
		Satisfied	Dissatisfied	Satisfied	Dissatisfied
Mothers	S	28	2	24	2
	US	7	14	6	17
Fathers	S	26	4	23	2
	US	2	17	5	18

both the first year and third year extreme groups. The three schools are combined for this purpose but in fact the pattern of response is very consistent in each of the schools, including the comprehensive school. There is clearly, from an examination of this table, a very close relationship between parental satisfaction and success. When the groups are compared using χ^2 the difference is significant ($p = < \cdot 01$).

Satisfaction or dissatisfaction with school progress is undoubtedly a factor in the more general approval or disapproval felt by these parents towards their sons. An examination of the case studies, however, shows that for many parents this is by no means the whole picture. Rather, in many – although not all – cases the lack of progress at school was, as we indicated in an earlier chapter, only part of a general and very pervasive discipline problem. Unsuccessful boys tended to be difficult not only over homework but also over friends, staying out late and growing their hair long. Parents of such boys found much to criticize about their sons, even if they also found some things, like acts of generosity or thoughtfulness, or honesty, for which they were ready to give praise.

In the case of those parents rated in the low approval category, they were so critical of their sons that they could find nothing to praise. In a few cases these parents, and particularly the fathers, could only be described as hostile. One such boy had been the focus of rows and scenes for several years, some over his school work, others of a more general kind. His father, who was particularly critical, found him erratic and careless and resentful of authority. He complained that his son was deceitful, and the boy had been thrashed severely on at least one occasion for lying. Yet another boy had run away from home after being beaten by his father for cheekiness. There were frequent rows in this family over friends and television as well as homework, and the mother described the father as 'always on at him'. Both these mothers were upset at the relationship between father and son, although they seemed to be unable to intervene successfully in the situation.

Parents of successful boys were rarely critical. One father, however, a professional man, was deeply disappointed that his son was attending the comprehensive school rather than one of the prestige grammar schools in the town. Although the boy according to our definition was doing well, the father saw him as an academic failure. Most of the heavy criticism of this boy was centred on his supposed failure at school, although there were also 'nasty rows' over answering back. The boy's choice of friends was also a problem. More typically, however, the parents of successful boys were very ready to express their pride and satisfaction. 'Nothing not to be proud of,' said the parents of one such boy, 'we can coax him to do anything.' Indeed, parents in this group tended to stress the good behaviour of their sons just as the parents of unsuccessful boys stressed bad behaviour. 'Not often naughty' or 'never a naughty child' and 'a very responsible boy' were typical of these comments. The phrase 'a child you can talk to' also expressed the happy relationship that existed between these parents and their sons. In general, for this group, although the parents were certainly very proud of their sons' success at school this was only a part of a pattern of behaviour in which conformity to parental rules and acceptance of parental values played a large part. Where such parents were critical, it was often for untidiness, or for not keeping shoes clean. Problems with friends, with the length of hair and with staying out late were rare in this group.

The warm relationships in these families must be seen, therefore, as in part at least a reaction to the boys' own behaviour. These boys were easy to handle and, according to their parents' accounts, had always been easy. On the other hand it is also possible, although we have no evidence on this, that the establishment of a warm loving background in the early years had itself been a factor in the development of the boys' co-operative attitudes and desire to please their parents. Further than this we are unable to go, but it does suggest that the relationship between parental warmth and approval and school achievement is not a simple cause and effect relationship.

The final rating on this particular dimension was given on the amount of sensitivity shown by parents to the needs of the child. High ratings were given when there was evidence of a close relationship and considerable intimacy between the parent and the child, and the parent concerned showed awareness of the child as an individual. Low ratings were given when there was evidence of lack of understanding and knowledge of the child.

An example of a family where both parents were rated as high on sensitivity is that of Paul Manners, a successful boy at the traditional grammar school. The family, as a group, shared many activities, including outings, concerts, etc., and the father used frequently to take the boy swimming. They were rated by the interviewer as a 'close family'. The parents described the boy as 'very open' in his relationship with them, and they for their part were willing to accept his fears, for example of the dark, with understanding and sympathy. Another example of high intimacy is provided by the parents of John Porter, another successful boy, but this time at a comprehensive school. These parents were aware of his problems at school, particularly of bullying. They frequently talked over homework with him and he often asked for their help, although they could no longer give any real assistance. They did not feel he ever asked for help unnecessarily and the interviewer reported that 'both parents seemed to enjoy being asked and included'. There was a close relationship with the father who would often 'fight and fool around with him'.

An example of an unsuccessful boy whose parents were rated high on sensitivity is Donald Robinson, a pupil at the technical grammar school. His parents, although aware of and worried about his lack of success, tended to put the blame on the teachers rather than on the boy himself. They were distressed at the rows that occurred over homework and the tension this produced in the home but were unsure of the best way to react to the situation, particularly since the father did not believe in forcing the son against his will. They had not visited the school about his bad reports as the boy had pleaded with them not to go and they felt that 'the boy suffers if the parents are difficult'. Although, therefore, clearly unable to accept their son's failure at school, these parents, like some others in their position, responded not with anger and rejection but with an attempt within their limitations to understand what had gone wrong and to do their best to put it right.

Ratings for low intimacy were given to parents who consistently refused help, and where the boys' problems were met with rejection rather than sympathy. One such boy was described by the interviewer as having an unhappy relationship with his father who would hit him when he was unhappy 'to knock some sense into him' and teach him to stand up for himself. A number of fathers of both successful and unsuccessful boys refused to give help in order to encourage independence or discourage what they saw as weakness. As one father put it, 'if you encourage them too much they rely too much on you.' In a few cases the father could only speak of the boy with dislike and contempt, and father and son did their best to avoid each other.

Table 4.4 gives the ratings for parental sensitivity for both mother and father, and for both first year and third year extreme groups. For the purpose of this table all three schools have been combined, although there were differences between schools, in that parents at the traditional grammar school were most likely and parents at the comprehensive school least likely to be given a high rating. This may reflect nothing more than a greater verbal facility on the part of the traditional grammar school parents which was very noticeable in the interviews. On the other hand it may be a reflection of real differences in parental behaviour arising out of the varying social class composition of

Table 4.4 *Parents' ratings for sensitivity: first and third year extreme groups*

Parent	Success category	1st year groups			3rd year groups		
		High rating	Inter-mediate rating	Low rating	High rating	Inter-mediate rating	Low rating
Mothers	S	15	17	1	10	14	5
	US	5	15	7	7	13	9
Fathers	S	14	13	6	10	11	8
	US	5	10	13	6	10	13

the three schools. This possibility will be discussed later. In the table there is a tendency for parental sensitivity according to our method of rating to be related to success. This tendency was more marked for the first year groups for both mothers and fathers. Using χ^2 the differences between the successful and unsuccessful boys was significant in the case of the first year extreme groups ($p = < \cdot 01$) but not in the case of the third year extreme groups.

Because both demonstration of affection and sensitivity as we have defined it appear to be measures of different kinds of intimacy, we examined the relationship between the ratings for fathers' demonstration of affection and both mothers' and fathers' sensitivity, using χ^2. The ratings for mothers' demonstration of affection were not included since they did not discriminate sufficiently. Each of the other three items were however found to be significantly related to each of the others, and the scores for all three items were accordingly combined into what we have called a 'nature of relationship' cluster score.[1] This cluster score was then related to success/unsuccess for the third year extreme groups, using analysis of variance.[2] When this was done, it was found that the relationships for the unsuccessful groups were less warm and close in each school, particularly at the grammar school. This was only marginally so at the comprehensive school. The differences between the successful and unsuccessful groups overall were not sufficiently large to reach the level of statistical significance (F ratio = 2·93).

The mothers' and fathers' ratings on pride and approval were also found to be related to each other, using χ^2.[3] They were combined in a parental approval cluster score. This cluster score was then related to success/unsuccess for the third year extreme groups, again using analysis of variance.[4] Parental approval was then found to be related to success, the pattern being similar in all three schools (F ratio = 8·08, p = < ·01). Parents at the comprehensive school showed somewhat less approval than

[1] The χ^2 values for this cluster will be found in appendix 3, p. 206.
[2] See appendix 4, Table A4.1, p. 227.
[3] For the χ^2 values see appendix 3, p. 206.
[4] See appendix 4, Table A4.2, p. 227.

other parents, but the difference between schools was not significant. The least approving group were the parents of unsuccessful boys at the technical grammar school.

The mothers' and fathers' responses to the item on satisfaction with school progress were also found to be interrelated,[1] using χ^2, and the scores were accordingly combined to form a parental satisfaction with school progress cluster. The scores were then related to success/unsuccess for the third year extreme groups using analysis of variance.[2] The pattern of scores is very consistent in all three schools, and significantly related to success $(F = 27·65, p = < ·001)$.

The three sets of scores falling into what we have defined, loosely, as the love/hostility dimension of parent/child relationships will be taken up again. The interrelationship of these three scores with each other and, even more importantly, with the scores on personality and motivation obtained from the boys and described in the two preceding chapters will be examined in a subsequent chapter (see pp. 126–31). In the meantime it is necessary to look at the second dimension of parent/child relationships to be examined in this study, that of the control/autonomy dimension.

4 THE CONTROL/AUTONOMY DIMENSION

Because of the complexity of parental behaviour along this dimension, and the difficulties of assessment, it was decided to approach it along a very broad front. We wanted to cover the amount of parental control, the area over which such control was exercised, and the methods of discipline employed. Moreover we needed to do this in such a way that 'conventional' replies would be minimized. The fact that we were more interested in behaviour than attitudes also made our task more complex. The methods we finally arrived at must therefore be regarded as experimental and not all our endeavours can be considered as successful. Nevertheless it was hoped that by using a variety of measures some of the difficulties inherent in the assessment of this kind of relationship would be avoided or at least minimized

[1] See appendix 3, p. 206.
[2] See appendix 4, Table A4.3, p. 228.

In order to make some assessment in behavioural terms of the amount of parental control, a series of questions was put to each family interviewed, all dealing with the exercise of parental control in areas which would appear to be significant for adolescent boys. The areas selected were friends, TV programmes, staying out late in the evening, hairstyles and homework. Parents were asked if they had any rules in each of these particular areas, what the rules were, what happened if the rules were disobeyed and the attitude of the boys to these rules. A question was also included on parental reaction to 'answering back'. From the answers to these questions we assessed the parents in terms of amount of control, and these assessments were then considered in relationship to the first year and third year extreme groups of successful and unsuccessful boys.

This process yielded no relationship between success and the amount of parental control as measured by this particular assessment, since both high and low parental control were distributed more or less equally between parents of successful and unsuccessful boys. An examination of the interviews themselves, however, indicated the strong possibility that the absence of parental rules was itself the product of different family situations. As we have already noted, many parents of succesful boys told us that their son did not need rules or control; he sat down to his homework of his own accord; he did not want to stay out late or grow his hair long; he never or rarely answered back. In short, these boys appeared to have internalized parental standards, and discipline was self-imposed. At the other extreme were those parents of unsuccessful boys who had given up trying to influence their son's behaviour. Other parents made only ineffective and sporadic attempts at control, e.g. nagging, which the boy appeared to ignore. The absence of control, in these cases, seemed largely an acknowledgement of defeat. On the other hand some parents of unsuccessful boys attempted a high level of control and met disobedience or rebellion with severe disciplinary measures. In one such case the interviewer was told that all of the three boys in the family were smacked on the spot if they came in late, and the TV was switched on only when the parent chose. Suspicion of smoking was punished by a severe thrashing, and homework was supervised strictly. Open disobedience was, therefore, very difficult for this child, and he responded by sullenness and lies. Moreover, although he was made to sit over his homework, the school complained that he did not do it properly. In another similar case beatings and thrashings were frequent, and on one occasion the father made his son eat two cigarettes as a punishment for smoking. This boy too responded with sullenness and on one occasion ran away from home. These were extreme cases but this pattern of strict parents and lack of success at school was repeated in several other families. Some parents of successful boys also appeared to be strict disciplinarians and, although homework was rarely a problem, rudeness or answering back was quite often the focus of family rows. Lack of tidiness or cleanliness and quarrels with siblings were other areas of parental concern in this group. On the whole, however, and unlike the unsuccessful boys, these boys were obedient and over a wide range of behaviour appeared to accept their parents' wishes. Strictness alone, therefore, does not relate to school success or failure.

It would seem, therefore, that the extent to which parents are controlling depends both on the extent to which such control is necessary, and on the desire for obedience. Although some boys needed more control than others, faced with disobedience some parents resorted to even sterner punishment while others virtually abdicated from any kind of control. Such an interpretation not only illustrates the complexity of this dimension of parental behaviour but also provides an interactional context for Bronfenbrenner's view of the curvilinear nature of the effects of discipline.

Our second approach to the control/autonomy question involved the use of a questionnaire designed to measure authoritarian/democratic attitudes. Twenty-nine items were included,[1] some from Schaefer and Bell's Parental Attitude Research Instrument[2] and others from a parental attitude questionnaire

[1] An item analysis was carried out but all items were retained. The split-half reliability, corrected by the Spearman-Brown formula and obtained from a sample of fifty schedules, was .86.

[2] E. S. Schaefer and R. Q. Bell, 'Development of a parental attitude research instrument', *Child Development*, XXIX (1958), pp. 339-61.

by Salmon.[1] The parents were asked to indicate whether they strongly agreed, agreed, were uncertain, disagreed, or strongly disagreed with each of the statements, examples of which are given below:

(a) a child has his own point of view and ought to be allowed to express it
(b) it is sometimes necessary for the parents to break a child's will
(c) there should be more discipline in school today.

The questionnaire was administered to the random sample of parents by postal questionnaire, and to the parents of the extreme groups of successful and unsuccessful boys at the time of the parental interviews. Unfortunately a high proportion of parents did not complete the questionnaire, and the response rate for the random sample in particular was only 78 per cent. For this reason the findings must be approached with some caution.

When the mean scores of mothers and fathers in the random sample were compared it was found that, although the fathers were slightly more authoritarian, the difference was not significant. One-way analysis of variance of these data also indicated that the differences between schools for both mothers' and fathers' responses were not significant. This is particularly interesting because of the differences between schools in social class background and parental education, which might have led us to expect some difference, particularly between the traditional grammar school and the rest.

In order to examine the relationship between parental democratic/authoritarian attitudes and school achievement for the extreme groups, the 't' test was used, since the low response of parents made it impossible to use analysis of variance. The parents, and particularly the mothers, of successful boys in both the traditional grammar and technical grammar schools tended to be more democratic in their attitudes than parents of unsuccessful boys, although only in the traditional grammar school

[1] Phillida Salmon, 'Differential conforming as a developing process', *British Journal of Social and Clinical Psychology*, VIII (1969), pp. 22–31.

was the difference significant (p = ·05).[1] The means of the two groups in the comprehensive school were very close for both mothers and fathers. Using all the data obtained from the random sample, correlations were run between parental autocratic attitudes and the boys' success categories.[2] Fathers and mothers in each of the schools were treated separately. As in the case of the extreme groups, the only significant one appeared in the grammar school when mothers expressing autocratic attitudes had unsuccessful sons.

These findings appear to give limited support to the thesis that school achievement is associated with democratic rather than authoritarian attitudes in parents, with mothers appearing as possibly more important than fathers. Since no such relationship was found when we examined the actual behaviour of parents, as reported by them in an interview, the meaning of this finding is not at all clear. The fact that the relationship between parental attitudes and school achievement did not appear in the comprehensive school must also be noted.

The third method used in this study to examine the autonomy/control dimension was the method of discipline customarily in use in the home. In order to assess this a series of open-ended questions was designed to elicit from the parents descriptions of the main disciplinary techniques used both to reward or encourage and to punish the child. Parents were first asked to name the kinds of things they encouraged in their children, and then to describe how they did this. This was followed by similar questions on punishment. If smacking had not been mentioned, parents were asked a number of supplementary questions on smacking. Interviewers were instructed to get from the parents as much detail as possible about actual examples, both of the child's behaviour and the response of the parent. It was hoped that this method of getting information, by focusing upon actual and often recent events, and by trying to get as much concrete description as possible, would not only help the more inarticulate parents, but would also make

[1] See appendix 4, Table A4.4, p. 228.
[2] See appendix 4, Table A4.5, p. 228.

it more difficult for the articulate ones to give conventional responses. The extra questions on smacking were included in case parents were unwilling to admit that they smacked their children.

The actual techniques mentioned by parents were then listed and classified into six types of control, four of them mainly 'physical' and two 'psychological'. Parents were then rated, according to whether they appeared to make use of each method of control or not, except in the case of smacking, where there were enough data to code parents on a five-point scale ranging from 'smacks frequently now' to 'has never smacked'. The possible relationship of these responses to school achievement was then examined for both the first year and third year extreme groups, using χ^2. One of the so-called 'physical' or 'material' methods of control used very frequently by parents was what they themselves described as 'threats' and sometimes as 'nagging' or 'shouting'. Since the threats were usually of smacking, or of deprivation of some material privilege, these answers were all grouped together in one category. Table 4.5 gives the responses of both mothers and fathers in each of the extreme groups but with all the schools combined.

There was a consistent tendency for parents of unsuccessful sons to be more likely to threaten, shout and grumble than parents of successful sons, although the majority of parents did actually make use of this method. The tendency was more

Table 4.5 *Parental threats, etc. as a method of control: first and third year extreme groups*

Parent	Success category	1st year groups		3rd year groups	
		Yes	No	Yes	No
Mothers	S	18	16	13	16
	US	21	9	21	7
Fathers	S	15	18	15	14
	US	16	13	20	9

marked in the case of the third year extreme groups, although only in the case of mothers was the relationship significant (p = < ·05).

Although coded on a five-point scale, the responses of the parents to the items on smacking have been grouped for the purpose of this analysis into frequent smacking and infrequent smacking and the responses, in this grouping, are set out in Table 4.6 for both the first year and third year extreme groups.

Table 4.6 *Frequency of smacking: first and third year extreme groups*

Parent	Success category	1st year groups		3rd year groups	
		Frequent	Infrequent	Frequent	Infrequent
Mothers	S	13	20	12	17
	US	18	10	19	9
Fathers	S	18	15	12	17
	US	18	10	17	12

Infrequent smacking was consistently related to success for both the first year and third year extreme groups, although only in the case of mothers in the third year extreme groups was the relationship significant (p = < ·05).

Another type of control mentioned by parents and classified by us as 'physical' or 'material' was the use of a tangible reward for good behaviour. These rewards usually took the form of pocket money, books, sweets, toys or outings and were used quite extensively by some parents, although others rejected the whole idea of 'reward' for good behaviour. There was, however, no tendency for this method of control to be used more by parents of either successful or unsuccessful boys. Nevertheless when parents used the deprivation of these same tangible objects as a punishment a different pattern emerged. There was now, as Table 4.7 shows, a marked tendency for the use of such material deprivation to be related to lack of success, a tendency which was significant (p = < ·05) in the case of the third year extreme groups.

D

Table 4.7 *Parental use of material deprivation: first and third*
year extreme groups

Parent	Success category	1st year groups		3rd year groups	
		Yes	No	Yes	No
Mothers	S	13	21	4	23
	US	15	15	13	15
Fathers	S	13	21	6	21
	US	16	14	14	15

The responses of the parents to a question on how they re-
acted when their sons answered back were coded into threat,
shout, smack on the one hand, and no action or verbal action of
one kind or another. Parents of boys in the third year extreme
groups were less likely to react with shouts, smacking, etc.,
perhaps because the boys were now two years older and answering back was taken less seriously. This kind of response was also
found more frequently among parents of unsuccessful boys in
the third year extreme groups. In the case of the first year
extreme groups where the majority of parents responded to
answering back in this way there was no relationship with success. Table 4.8 gives the parental reaction for both sets of extreme groups.

Table 4.8 *Parental reaction to answering back: first and third year*
extreme groups

Success category	1st year groups		3rd year groups	
	Verbal or no action	Shouts, smacks, etc.	Verbal or no action	Shouts, smacks, etc.
S	15	18	24	5
US	11	17	16	13

Two further categories of analysis – the use of approval and
praise as a reward and the use of disapproval or rejection as a

punishment – showed no consistent pattern of relationship with success. This may have been because of the difficulty of securing accurate information on the use made by parents of this method of control, since it may well have been operated by many of them in an unconscious way. There was, however, a tendency for fathers of successful boys, in the third year extreme group only, to be more likely to use approval as a method of control.

The next step was to examine the items on parental discipline using χ^2, to see if they were themselves related. Eight items were included in this analysis, namely, parental reaction to answering back, mothers' and fathers' use of threats, frequency of smacking, material deprivation and fathers' use of pride and approval.[1] The two items on parental reaction to answering back and fathers' use of approval were not found to be related to the rest, but the other six items were all found to be interrelated, suggesting that within certain families there is a particular pattern of discipline in which smacking, shouting and threatening, and material deprivation are the typical method of control. In order to examine further the relationship between this pattern of control and success at school, the scores for the three methods of discipline were combined and the cluster score was related to success for the third year extreme groups only, using analysis of variance.[2] When this was done, it was found that mothers of successful boys in all the schools consistently made less use of these material or 'non-psychological' forms of control ($F = 9.95$ $p = < .01$). Mothers in the comprehensive school also made more use of these methods than other mothers, although the difference between schools is not significant. Fathers of successful boys were also less likely than fathers of unsuccessful boys to use material or non-psychological methods of control ($F = 4.20$, $p = < .05$) but the pattern is less consistent.

It seems therefore that particularly in the two grammar schools the use of material or non-psychological methods of control was related to lack of success, although once again the precise causal pattern is not easy to disentangle. It is at least possible that the greater severity of punishment found among

[1] For the χ^2 values see appendix 3, pp. 206–7.
[2] See appendix 4, Tables A 4.6–7, p. 229.

parents of unsuccessful boys is related to the higher incidence of problems they have had with their sons, and it may be that these boys for some reason have always been more difficult to handle. Alternatively, it is equally consistent with our data that the use by these parents of non-psychological forms of punishment has itself produced the less conformist personalities of their sons. According to this interpretation the lack of success at school is only one aspect of a general failure to internalize parental desires and parental standards. It is to a consideration of this possibility that we must now turn.

In reviewing the literature on parental disciplinary techniques it was pointed out that coercive methods of discipline, including the use of physical punishment, do not appear to be favourable to the development of conscience, that is the internalization of parental expectations and demands. Indeed, the internalization process seems to be most successful in a family environment where relationships between parents and children are warm and affectionate, but where the use of approval and disapproval as disciplinary techniques evokes a fear of the loss of love. If this is so, then the techniques favoured by the parents of successful boys have been a factor in producing the acceptance of and conformity to standards which we have already noticed as a highly significant aspect of the boys' personality from the point of view of their high achievement at school. Moreover an examination of the case study material provides evidence of such a relationship between the method of discipline, the warmth of the family relationship and the response of the child. The parents of successful and also conformist boys would report that they had not smacked for years, that the tone of voice or the expression on the face was enough. According to one such father, 'he listens and watches if he pleases us; then he's made up'. At the other extreme we have already noted the combination of cold and even hostile fathers and the frequent use of physical punishment, resentment and even open rebellion on the part of the son, and increasing failure at school. All of this suggests an interrelationship between patterns of child-rearing, personality development and school achievement which will be explored more fully in a later chapter.

CHAPTER FIVE

SOCIAL CLASS AND SCHOOL ACHIEVEMENT

1 THE PROBLEM STATED

In choosing to focus, in the first instance, upon the individual pupil, no attention has as yet been paid to the very considerable literature on the relationship between school achievement and social class. It is to this relationship and its implications for our study that we must now turn if we are to extend our understanding of the process of school success or failure, and in particular of the way in which patterns of child-rearing are influenced by position within the social structure.

The concept of social class is itself highly complex, and its use raises a number of issues of considerable theoretical and practical importance which will need to be considered at a later stage (see pp. 178–82). In the meantime it is useful to begin by looking at those studies which have examined particular indices of social class or socio-economic status and their relationship to various measures of school achievement, and of these the obvious starting point is occupational status. Although the use of occupation as an indicator of social class has been rightly criticized, it can be defended on the grounds of its convenience, since it is information which is relatively simple to collect and to code. At the same time, and in spite of notable exceptions, it is closely linked to income on the one hand and to social status, or prestige, on the other, so that it seems to summarize these two major aspects of socio-economic status more than any other single measure. Moreover the different life chances and life experiences typical of certain occupational groupings may well predispose them towards a different view of the world and of their place in it.[1]

The very consistent relationship between father's occupation and school achievement at all levels of the educational system with the possible exception of higher education has frequently been summarized[2] and is now too well known to need repeating here. From the point of view of this particular study, however, it is necessary to bear in mind that father's occupation has been found to relate not only to 11-plus success but also to progress within the grammar school itself. This relationship has been shown to persist, moreover, when measured ability has been controlled.

Although the occupation of the father is the more usual measure of the family's status, mother's occupation before marriage has also been included in a few studies, and there is some evidence that it operates as an independent variable, particularly in influencing working-class success. For example, Floud, Halsey and Martin's study[3] found that those mothers whose occupation before marriage was superior to that of their husbands were more likely than other mothers to have children who were successful in the 11-plus. The social origin of the parents themselves has also attracted some attention, and again there is some evidence that the children of those working-class parents who have been downwardly mobile are more likely to be high achievers than other working-class children.

Although occupation plays a very central role in studies of social class and educability, most researches have made use of additional indices which can be considered to be aspects of social class or socio-economic status. These are sometimes treated as separate factors, and sometimes incorporated with occupation

[1] See for example D. G. McKinley, *Social Class and Family Life* (Glencoe, Illinois, The Free Press, 1964).

See for example Olive Banks, *The Sociology of Education* (London, Batsford, 1971), chapters 3, 4, 5.

J. Floud, A. H. Halsey and F. Martin, *Social Class and Educational Opportunity* (London, Heinemann, 1956).

into a single measure. One factor which has been treated in this way is the economic or material circumstances of the family. There is evidence in support of the assumption that the lower school performance of some working-class children is affected by their poor material development, although the Floud, Halsey and Martin study suggests that the effect of such an environment may well operate only below a certain threshold.[1] Poverty, moreover, may achieve its influence on school achievement in a variety of ways. Sexton,[2] for example, has shown that children from poor homes are handicapped directly by higher rates of sickness and poor rates of attendance. Bad housing, itself a concomitant of poverty, also appears to handicap school achievement,[3] but here the effect may well be indirect. Its influence on achievement may be mediated by its impact on the quality of family life, on patterns of child-rearing and on family relationships generally. On the other hand, poverty may have an inhibiting effect on ambition and, through this factor, on achievement. This possibility may be particularly important at the secondary school where staying on beyond the school leaving age or going on to higher education imposes a financial sacrifice on both the child and the parent. Poverty, especially when it takes the form of long-term financial insecurity, may also have an influence on value orientations. Families who have known such insecurity for perhaps generations are not likely to develop a belief in their ability to control their environment or to plan for the future. Clearly, therefore, the relationship between material environment and school achievement is a complex one, and can only finally be understood in interaction with other aspects of family life.

Another cognate area which has been very extensively researched and amply documented is the relationship between measured ability and family size. The large family is, to some extent, part of the 'culture of poverty' and there is a relationship between the size of family and socio-economic status. On the

[1] ibid.
[2] P. Sexton, *Education and Income* (New York, Viking, 1961).
[3] J. W. B. Douglas, *The Home and the School* (London, MacGibbon and Kee, 1964).

other hand the effect of family size on intelligence appears to operate at all socio-economic levels, even if not to the same extent in the middle classes.[1] Nevertheless the process by which family size influences ability is still largely unexplored, although both the material consequences for housing standards and the amount and kind of parent/child interaction are promising areas of study.

Like occupation, level of parental education is a convenient index of socio-economic status and is sometimes used in combination with income and occupation for this purpose. Its relationship to school achievement is too well documented to need reviewing here. As with the other indices discussed so far, however, there is still a need to spell out the process by which the educational background of the parent influences the school progress of the child. Clearly a direct link is feasible between the intellectual level of the parents and the 'educability' of the home, which can express itself in such practical ways as helping with homework as well as in shared hobbies of an 'intellectual' kind, and in a greater pressure for educational success. The indirect effects of educational background are also likely to be pervasive since the level of education can manifest itself throughout the whole style or way of life. Consequently a full examination of its influence would need to include a consideration not only of linguistic styles and their transmission but of the whole pattern of parent-child interaction. It follows therefore that the educational level of the parents may be a decisive influence in all the differences in parental values and parental behaviour that we have examined in previous chapters.

If the explanation of the relationship between social class differences in school achievement is to be sought in differences in parental values and parental behaviour, then it must be established that the main social classes do indeed differ in these particular ways. While this area has been less extensively researched, particularly in this country, there is evidence that working-class parents have lower educational aspirations than middle-class parents. The latter are, for example, more likely to prefer a grammar school to a secondary modern school, tend

[1] Douglas, *The Home and the School.*

to prefer a later school leaving age and tend to have higher occupational aspirations for their children. It is argued, too, that middle-class parents take more interest in their children's progress at school.[1] Whether the lower aspirations of working-class parents are part of a distinctive set of value orientations which place a low value on achievement, or whether they simply reflect a process of adjustment to circumstances is however still very much a matter of debate.

There has also been some research into social class differences in child-rearing, with fairly consistent findings. In general, middle-class parents have been shown to be more likely to use love-oriented or psychological methods of discipline. Working-class parents, on the other hand, are more likely to use ridicule, shouting or physical punishment in disciplining the child.[2] Most of these studies have been carried out in the United States, but their findings are generally confirmed by the Newsons in their interviews of Nottingham parents. They found that middle-class mothers of 4 year olds preferred the use of reasoning and explanation, whereas the working-class mothers were more likely to resort to authority and the child's respect for adults.[3]

Although the early work of Bernstein was mainly on children's speech, his more recent research has included studies of mothers' use of communication and control which demonstrate social class differences in the process of socialization. Middle-class mothers, for example, were found to be more likely to take up the child's attempts at conversation, and less likely to avoid or evade difficult questions, less likely to use coercive, threatening or imperative forms of control and more likely to value the educational use of toys.[4]

It might be argued therefore that working-class children are

[1] ibid. See also Plowden Report: Report of the Central Advisory Council for Education (England), *Children and their Primary Schools* (London, HMSO, 1967).
[2] See for example D. R. Miller and G. R. Swanson, *Inner Conflict and Defence* (New York, Henry Holt, 1960).
[3] J. Newson and E. Newson, *Four Years Old in an Urban Community* (London, Allen and Unwin, 1968).
[4] W. Brandis and D. Henderson, *Social Class, Language and Communication* (London, Routledge and Kegan Paul, 1970).

less likely than middle-class children to internalize parental standards. In line with this is the finding that working-class children are more likely than middle-class children to evaluate an act in terms of its consequences rather than its intent.[1] Moreover Kohn found that working-class parents were more likely than middle-class parents to value conformity to external prescription and less likely to value the development of internalized standards of conduct.[2] There is some evidence therefore for the view that those differences in the socialization process which appear to be important for school achievement are rooted in the differing life experiences of different social groupings.

On the other hand we should beware of too deterministic a view of the effect of social class on achievement. There are important inter-class as well as intra-class differences, and working-class children who are successful at school are worthy of more detailed study than they have as yet received. One of the most frequent inter-class distinctions which has been made is in terms of occupational skill, and it has been shown several times that the children of skilled workers perform better at school than the children of the unskilled. In some studies the children of foremen do better than those of other manual workers.[3] Another factor which has been singled out for attention is the effect of downward mobility, or what Jackson and Marsden call the sunken middle class.[4] There is some evidence that the children of those working-class families who have experienced downward mobility in their own or a previous generation are more likely to do well at school.[5] Another similar approach to the problem is through the concept of blocked mobility. Kahl, for example, found that the fathers of his high achievers were often unhappy or dissatisfied with their occupational status whereas the fathers of his under-achievers, although in a similar

[1] L. Boehm and M. L. Nass, 'Social class differences in conscience development', *Child Development*, XXXIII (1962), pp. 565–74.
[2] M. L. Kohn, 'Social class and parental values', *American Journal of Sociology*, LXIV (1959), pp. 337–51.
[3] See for example J. Floud, A. H. Halsey and F. Martin, op. cit.
[4] B. Jackson and D. Marsden, *Education and the Working Class* (London, Routledge and Kegan Paul, 1962).
[5] ibid.

socio-economic grouping, were content to 'get by'.[1] Another, and rather different approach is taken by Toomey[2] who, in a recent study, looked at expenditure on the home within a group of working-class families with similar incomes. He found that families with high as compared with low expenditure on the home showed a greater degree of interest and participation in their children's education, and this was associated with higher educational attainment on the part of the child.

While these studies indicate certain areas in which further research might be undertaken, they do not in themselves take us very far in understanding intra-class differences in achievement. This is partly because in most cases the method of study does not allow us to go beyond the structural variables like level of skill or social class origin to a direct examination of the way of life of the families involved. Yet working-class success would seem to be a necessary part of a study of working-class achievement. In discussing the findings of this research in so far as they relate to social class or socio-economic status, particular attention therefore will be paid to the successful working-class child.

2 SOCIO-ECONOMIC STATUS AND SCHOOL ACHIEVEMENT: THE FINDINGS

In describing the three secondary schools chosen for this study, the point has already been made[3] that there were considerable differences between them not only with respect to pupil ability as measured by 11-plus quotients but also in the socio-economic status of the parents. Father's occupation was used as the main index of socio-economic status, and was coded, using the Registrar General's Occupational Classification, into four non-manual and four manual categories. Since the numbers in the sample were small, foremen were included in the skilled manual category. Table 5.1 shows the proportions of boys with fathers in non-manual and manual occupations in each of the schools for

[1] J. Kahl, op. cit.
[2] D. M. Toomey, 'Home-centred working class parents' attitudes towards their son's education and career', *Sociology* III (3) (1969).
[3] See the discussion on pp. 7–9.

the random sample of boys interviewed during the boys' final year at school. The numbers in brackets represent the actual numbers in the sample. In all the schools combined, 32 per cent

Table 5.1 *The proportion of fathers in non-manual and manual occupations in the three schools*

School	Non-manual		Manual	
	%	No.	%	No.
Traditional grammar	48	(22)	52	(24)
Grammar technical	34	(14)	66	(27)
Comprehensive	10	(4)	90	(34)
All schools	32	(40)	68	(85)

or roughly a third of the boys had fathers in non-manual occupations, but there is considerable difference between schools, and non-manual families are virtually unrepresented in the comprehensive school.

It is against this background that we must examine the relationship between fathers' occupation and our extreme groups of successful and unsuccessful boys within each school. Table 5.2 gives this information for both the first year and third year extreme groups.

The tendency for successful boys to have fathers in non-manual occupations is completely consistent, although it is only statistically significant, using χ^2, in the traditional grammar school (p = < ·05). On the other hand, bearing in mind the small proportion of non-manual fathers in the other schools, and particularly in the comprehensive school, the consistency of the results is surprising. Moreover in each school the trend is slightly more marked for the third year than for the first year extreme groups. When all schools are combined the difference for the third year groups is significant (p = < ·01) and it is particularly striking that in this group there are only four boys with fathers in non-manual occupations who are in the unsuccessful group.

All the mothers interviewed were asked their occupation before marriage, and the distribution for the random sample is

Table 5.2 *Fathers' occupation in the extreme groups of successful and unsuccessful boys*

School	Success category	1st year extreme groups		3rd year extreme groups	
		Non-manual	Manual	Non-manual	Manual
Traditional grammar	S	9	4	9	2
	US	3	7	2	7
Grammar technical	S	3	7	3	5
	US	2	8	2	9
Comprehensive	S	2	8	4	6
	US	0	7	0	9
All schools	S	14	19	16	13
	US	5	22	4	25

given in Table 5.3. As for fathers, the classification is into manual and non-manual categories.

Table 5.3 *The proportion of mothers in non-manual and manual occupations in the three schools*

School	Non-manual		Manual	
	%	No.	%	No.
Traditional grammar	70	(31)	30	(13)
Grammar technical	52	(22)	48	(20)
Comprehensive	50	(16)	50	(16)
All schools	59	(69)	41	(49)

Wives were considerably more likely to have been in a non-manual job than their husbands in all three schools, although the pattern of differences is the same, with the most non-manual occupations at the traditional grammar school and the least at the comprehensive school. The significance of this finding is not clear, and it may represent no more than lower status of routine non-manual jobs for women than for men. This possibility is reinforced by the absence of any consistent pattern of relationship between mother's occupation and the extreme groups of successful and unsuccessful boys.[1] Boys with mothers in non-manual jobs were just as likely to be unsuccessful as successful in the third year extreme groups. For this reason no further analysis was made of mothers' occupational status.

All the parents interviewed were asked to give us the occupation of their own fathers during the time they were at school. Most parents were able to give us this information, which was coded in the same manner as parental occupation.

Table 5.4 gives the relationship between father's and *paternal* grandfather's occupation for the random sample of boys in each school, and Table 5.5 the relationship between father's and *maternal* grandfather's occupation for the same group of boys.

Table 5.4 *Paternal grandfather's occupation by father's occupation for the random sample of boys*

Paternal grandfather's occupation	Father's Occupation							
	Traditional grammar		Technical grammar		Compre-hensive		Combined	
	nm	*m*	*nm*	*m*	*nm*	*m*	*nm*	*m*
Non-manual	9	3	4	3	2	5	15	11
Manual	13	18	9	25	2	29	24	72

There is very little difference between the social origin of mothers and fathers. Some 22 per cent of paternal grandfathers and 18 per cent of maternal grandfathers had non-manual occupations. Eleven fathers (9 per cent) and twelve mothers (9 per cent) were sunken-middle-class whereas twenty-four fathers (20 per cent) and twenty-eight mothers (21 per cent) had been occupationally mobile. It will be noticed also that only fifteen (12 per cent) of the present non-manual families had paternal grand-

[1] See appendix 4, Table A5.1, p. 230.

Table 5.5 *Maternal grandfather's occupation by father's occupation for the random sample of boys*

Maternal grandfather's occupation	Father's Occupation							
	Traditional grammar		Technical grammar		Compre-hensive		Combined	
	nm	m	nm	m	nm	m	nm	m
Non-manual	9	4	2	4	0	4	11	12
Manual	12	20	12	24	4	30	28	74

fathers who were also in non-manual occupation, so that very few of our sample came from the established middle class. The largest groups of parents were working-class by both social origin and present occupation even in the traditional grammar school.

For the purpose of the analysis of the extreme groups where the total number was small, no attempt was made to differentiate between the sunken-middle-class and other families, or between the socially mobile and the non-mobile. Instead a comparison was made in terms of simple social origin so that all those with non-manual grandparents were compared with those whose grandparents were in manual occupation. Paternal and maternal grandparents were however kept separate. Table 5.6 shows the results of this analysis with all three schools combined.[1]

Table 5.6 *Grandfathers' occupation for first and third year extreme groups*

	Success category	1st year extreme groups		3rd year extreme groups	
		Non-manual	Manual	Non-manual	Manual
Paternal grandfather	S	18	15	12	17
	US	4	22	2	26
Maternal grandfather	S	6	23	8	20
	US	3	25	6	23

[1] See appendix 4, Tables A5.2–3, pp. 230–1.

There is a tendency for paternal grandfathers' occupation to be related to success and, for the third year extreme groups, when χ^2 is used, this is significant (p = < ·01). In the case of maternal grandfathers, the trend although in the same direction is very small, and there is in fact very little difference between the successful and unsuccessful boys. Our findings, therefore, do not support the view that the social background of the mother is of particular importance for school achievement, and, at least for this sample of boys, it is the father who appears to be the more important.

Occupational status is, however, only one aspect of social class, and additional information was also collected on the income of the family. Since the difficulty in the way of collecting accurate detailed information on income is well known, it was decided to get a fairly rough assessment by asking parents to put themselves into one of 5 categories ranging from below £500 to above £2000 per annum. Respondents were asked to include both husband's and wife's income, after tax, in 'take-home pay'. Very few respondents made any objections to giving this information, although of course we have no check of its accuracy. The distribution of the income of the random sample, by occupation, is given in Table 5.7. For convenience, the five income levels have been grouped into the two categories which give the most even response over all three schools.

As might be expected, income is closely related to occupation, and when χ^2 is used the difference is significant (p = < ·01). There are for this reason significant differences between schools, with income in the traditional grammar school higher than at either of the other two schools, although the difference between schools within the manual category is not very great. It is therefore quite surprising to see only a slight relationship between income and achievement when the first year and third year extreme groups[1] are compared, suggesting that the greater material prosperity of the non-manual families was not a very significant factor in their success. There is, it is true, a fairly consistent tendency for higher income to be related to success, but the relationship is at no time more than a very slight one,

[1] See appendix 4, Table A5.4, p. 231.

Table 5.7 *Income by occupation for the random sample of boys in each of the schools*

School	Father's occupation	Income	
		Below £1,000 p.a.	Above £1,000 p.a.
Traditional grammar	Non-manual	4	18
	Manual	15	9
Grammar technical	Non-manual	7	7
	Manual	24	3
Comprehensive	Non-manual	0	2
	Manual	26	10
Combined	Non-manual	11	27
	Manual	65	22

even in the traditional grammar school which had the highest proportion of non-manual families, and those families earning above £1000 per annum are almost as likely to be unsuccessful as they are to be successful.

An attempt was also made to measure housing conditions by using an index of overcrowding based on the size of the household and the number of bedrooms in the house. If the boy in question had to share a bedroom with more than one sibling, or with an adult, e.g. a grandparent, the house was rated as overcrowded. In fact, few houses were overcrowded according to this definition. In the third year extreme groups there were sixteen overcrowded families, only 28 per cent of the families in this group. Of these, seven were the homes of successful boys and nine the homes of unsuccessful boys. It would not appear, therefore, to be of any great importance so far as this particular study is concerned. Family size, too, was unrelated to success for our particular sample. Boys from one- to two-child families were almost as likely to be unsuccessful as successful in all three schools. Similarly boys from large families were almost as likely to be successful as unsuccessful.

In so far, therefore, as occupational status has been shown to be related to success, particularly in the traditional grammar school, it does not seem as if poverty and other material aspects of the environment were determining factors in the relationship. It should be borne in mind, however, that few of our families were living in extreme poverty, and although some of the housing was of poor quality, this was by no means the rule, and many of the families had been rehoused on new estates in the suburbs.

No relationship between family size and achievement was found.[1] This is surprising, but the most likely explanation lies in the relative homogeneity of family size within schools. Information obtained from the random sample of parents[2] showed that family size at the comprehensive school was significantly larger than at either of the other two schools. Moreover, within the comprehensive school itself family size is significantly smaller for the selective boys.[3] This confirms the relationship between family size and 11-plus success so far as our particular sample is concerned. There was also, when all three schools were combined, a relationship in the expected direction between family size and father's occupation, but *within* schools the relationship between the two was very small. At the traditional grammar school, for example, the mean number of siblings was 1·14 for the non-manual families and only 1·5 for the manual families. At the technical grammar school the mean for non-manual families was 1·07 and for manual families 1·88. This is a larger difference but is not statistically significant. At the comprehensive schools the non-manual family size was slightly larger. Working-class families were not, therefore, at a disadvantage with respect to family size within the comprehensive school, nor indeed to any extent in the traditional grammar school. It is necessary therefore to turn to other aspects of social class differences if we are to interpret our particular findings.

[1] See appendix 4, Tables A5.5–6, p. 232.
[2] See appendix 4, Table A5.6, p. 232.
[3] See appendix 4, Table A5.7, p. 232.

3 THE EDUCATIONAL LEVEL OF THE HOME

The suggestion has already been made that the educational background of the parents may have an influence on the child in a wide variety of ways, and one of the objects of our research was to explore some of the ways in which the level of parental education might take effect. Our first objective, however, was to discover the formal educational background of the parents in our sample, and to see how it was related to school achievement. For this purpose all the parents interviewed were asked a series of questions on their educational experiences. Table 5.8 gives the type of secondary school attended by fathers and mothers in the random sample, according to the occupational status of the father.

Table 5.8 *Parents' secondary education by occupational status for random sample*

School attended	Father's occupational status			
	Non-manual		Manual	
	Mother's education	Father's education	Mother's education	Father's education
Selective	7	15	14	10
Non-selective	31	24	71	76

The majority both of mothers (83 per cent) and fathers (80 per cent) had attended a non-selective school. Parents of boys at the traditional grammar school were more likely to have gone to a selective school than other parents, but the difference between schools was not as great as might have been expected bearing in mind the differences in occupational status between the schools.[1] In fact, although fathers in non-manual occupations were more likely to have had a selective education, the majority of fathers in

[1] See appendix 4, Tables A5.8–9, p. 233 for a comparison between schools.

in this category had been to a non-selective school. Another interesting feature is the lack of any real relationship between mothers' education and fathers' occupational status. Particularly striking in this connection is the disparity between mothers and fathers for those in the non-manual occupational category

It appears, therefore, that a grammar school education was outside the personal experience of the majority of parents even of those classified as 'middle-class'. Moreover, even those parents who had attended a selective school tended to leave relatively early and only three mothers and three fathers had stayed on at school after the age of sixteen. With these exceptions, therefore, even those parents who had been to a grammar school were without experience of a sixth form.

This picture of a very limited educational background for the majority of our sample is however somewhat modified when we look at the pattern of part-time and full-time further and higher education given in Table 5.9. For the purposes of this table, those parents who have had experience of both full-time and part-time further or higher education are classified in the full-time category only.[1]

Table 5.9 *Parents' further and higher education by occupational status for random sample*

| | Father's occupational status | | | |
| | Non-manual | | Manual | |
Type of education	Mother's education	Father's education	Mother's education	Father's education
Full-time	11	18	16	32
Part-time	5	16	13	17
None	24	6	58	36

[1] See appendix 4, Tables A5.10–13, pp. 233–4 for a comparison between schools.

Fathers in the non-manual category were more likely than other fathers to have had some form of further or higher education, but the majority, even of fathers in the manual category, had had some experience of further education. In the case of mothers, the situation was different, and as many as 65 per cent had had no further or higher education at all, compared with only 34 per cent of fathers. A further analysis in terms of length of educational experience indicates, however, that for many fathers the time spent on full-time further education was very short. Of the fifty fathers who claimed full-time further or higher education, thirty-one of them had been on courses of less than a year's duration, and most in fact had formed part either of army training or some kind of apprenticeship course. The full-time further education of mothers was similarly mostly in the form of short vocational courses, e.g. shorthand and typing. It was decided therefore to classify parents in terms of formal educational qualifications, since these might serve as an indicator of the 'weight' of the course. This information is given for both parents in Table 5.10. All qualifications are grouped together as there were not sufficient parents with such qualifications to justify a breakdown.

Table 5.10 *Parents' qualifications by father's occupation for the random sample*

| Qualifications | Father's occupational status | | | |
| | Non-manual | | Manual | |
	Mothers	Fathers	Mothers	Fathers
Yes	11	25	14	22
No	29	15	73	64

Some 37 per cent of fathers, but only 20 per cent of mothers, had a formal qualification. For fathers, in particular, educational qualifications were clearly linked to occupational status, and the majority of non-manual fathers in fact had a qualification of some kind. Although it was by no means rare for a manual father to have a formal qualification, such fathers were in a minority.

To summarize, therefore, fathers in the random sample have considerably more formal education than the mothers, and this appears to be particularly marked for the non-manual category. Socio-economic status as measured by fathers' occupation is related to the educational experience of the parents, but considerably less so in the case of the mothers. Much of the educational experience, of fathers particularly, is however of a vocational kind, and neither mothers nor fathers have much experience of a grammar school. This is true even of many whose occupational status places them as 'middle-class'.

It is now necessary to consider whether these differences in educational background are related to school achievement. Table 5.11 shows the secondary education of both mothers and fathers for the third year extreme groups of successful and unsuccessful boys.

Table 5.11 *Parents' secondary education: third year extreme groups*

School attended	Success category	Mothers	Fathers
Selective	S	8	11
	US	2	5
Non-selective	S	20	18
	US	27	24

The main difficulty in interpreting these findings is the small number of parents with a selective secondary education. There is a clear tendency for both mothers and fathers who had been to a selective secondary school to have successful rather than unsuccessful sons, but the item discriminates so badly that more of the highly successful group had parents who had been to an unselective than to a selective school. Only in the traditional grammar school is there a significant tendency ($p = < \cdot 01$) for fathers' secondary education to be related to sons' success.[1]

Experience of further or higher education was also related to the extreme groups. Because of the small numbers, the breakdown used was a simple one of some further education or none. Although there was a tendency for further education to be related to success the relationship, other than at the traditional grammar school, is not very great or very consistent.[2] This may reflect the fact that at the traditional grammar school further education was more likely to be of an advanced kind, and associated with a formal qualification.

Such formal educational experience is however only one way of measuring the educational background of the home, and a number of studies have attempted to assess it in a more direct way by looking at such variables as the reading habits of the parents, and their hobbies and interests. It is assumed, reasonably enough, that the parent who is interested in reading and has 'intellectual' interests is likely to provide an atmosphere in the home congenial to success in school. The interview with the random sample, accordingly, included a series of questions on parental interests and activities in order to assess what is sometimes termed the 'cultural' background of the home. Because of the importance given to it in the literature, parental reading habits were singled out for special attention, and parents were classified as regular readers if they claimed to have read a book during the month preceding the interview. Although our definition of 'regular' readers was a wide one, the majority of parents in the sample were classified as occasional or non-readers.[3] Only 41 per cent of the fathers were regular readers, and 32 per cent of the mothers. Fathers with sons at the traditional grammar school were more likely to be regular readers than other fathers and at this school the regular readers were in the majority, although even in this school 46 per cent were classified as occasional or non-readers. Mothers who were regular readers were in a minority in all schools. There was however little

[1] See appendix 4, Table A5.14, p. 235.
[2] See appendix 4, Table A5.15, p. 235.
[3] See appendix 4, Table A5.16, p. 236.

relationship between reading habits and fathers' occupation, and in the traditional grammar school fathers in manual occupations were just as likely to be regular readers as those in non-manual occupations.

Parents in the random sample were even less likely to be members of a library than to be regular readers, and this would appear to indicate quite a strong commitment to reading as a hobby. Some 30 per cent of fathers and 34 per cent of mothers claimed such membership, so that using this index of reading interest there is little difference between mothers and fathers.[1] There were no significant differences between schools, and in all schools the majority of parents were not members of a library. Nor was there any consistent relationship between library membership and fathers' occupation, and at the traditional grammar school manual fathers were *more* likely to be library members than non-manual fathers.

An attempt was also made to classify the type of magazine taken by each family into 'serious' journals and other journals. In fact the number of families taking serious magazines was quite high (50 per cent), although some may have been read by the sons rather than the parents. The families with sons at the traditional grammar schools were most likely to take such journals, and the difference between this school and the comprehensive school, using χ^2, was significant ($p = < \cdot 05$).[2] Manual families were less likely to take such journals than non-manual families in all schools, although the difference within schools was not significant. Manual families in the traditional grammar school were much more likely to take such journals than manual families in the comprehensive school ($p = < \cdot 05$).

The difference between schools, which is consistent throughout these measures, suggests that the 'cultural' background of the home is a significant factor in 11-plus success, since the proportion of homes with such a background is highest at the traditional grammar school, where 11-plus scores were also highest, and lowest at the comprehensive school, where 11-plus scores were also low. This finding is in line with previous research in

[1] See appendix 4, Table A5.17, p. 236.
[2] See appendix 4, Table A5.18, p. 236.

this area.[1] Of particular interest in this connection is the way in which manual fathers in the traditional grammar school have reading patterns which approximate more closely to those of the non-manual families than to those of other manual workers in the sample, and particularly those in the comprehensive school. This suggests that what we have defined as 'cultural' background may be an important factor in working-class 'success'. In order to test this, a set of questions on reading habits was given to the parents of both the first year and third year extreme groups of successful and unsuccessful boys. In order to simplify the analysis, a composite code was drawn up making use of all the items. Families were coded on a five-point scale which ranged from most serious to least serious readers, the highest score going to families where both parents were readers of what we classified as 'serious' books and magazines, and the lowest to those who read nothing but popular newspapers. Table 5.14 gives the distribution of scores for both the first year and third year extreme groups. For this purpose, codes 4 and 5 are grouped as serious readers, and 2 and 3 as non-serious readers.

Table 5.14 *Parents' reading scores: first year and third year extreme groups*

Success category	1st year extreme groups			3rd year extreme groups		
	Non-readers	Non-serious readers	Serious readers	Non-readers	Non-serious readers	Serious readers
Successful	9	17	10	9	11	9
Unsuccessful	18	14	0	13	11	1

Very few families have been classified as 'serious readers', although a large number are 'non-serious' readers, that is, one

[1] See for example E. Fraser, *Home Environment and the School* (University of London Press, 1959); Plowden Report, Report of the Central Advisory Council for Education (England), *Children and their Primary Schools* (London, HMSO, 1967).

or both parents read light fiction or women's magazines fairly regularly. Serious reading is almost entirely confined to the parents of successful sons, and the sons of non-readers are less likely to be in the successful group so that there is clearly a relationship between 'serious reading' on the part of the parents and school achievement. On the other hand in the third year extreme groups 'non-serious' readers are as likely to have unsuccessful as successful sons. Moreover in each of the successful groups a large minority of boys came from families classified as 'non-readers'. The relationship between reading habits and school achievement is, therefore, a complex one, and only what we have classified as habits of 'serious' reading appears to give any advantage. In the comprehensive school, where there is only one family in this category, there is no relationship between reading habits and success.[1]

As we have already argued, parental education is not itself a causal variable, and one of the ways in which it might be supposed to influence school achievement is by enabling the parents to help with homework. In order to determine how far help with homework was a factor in the school achievement of our sample we asked the parents of boys in the extreme successful and unsuccessful groups a series of questions on the amount and kind of help that was actually given with the boys' homework. Special attention was paid to mathematics and to foreign languages since these were areas which produced a large number of problems. It is appreciated that these replies may not be accurate, although by encouraging the parents to talk freely we hoped to avoid 'conventional' answers. Nor of course is this in any sense a measure of effective help.

In the case of the first year extreme groups, whose parents were interviewed during the boys' second year at the school, the majority were getting some help with their maths homework from their fathers.[2] Only twenty boys had had no help at all. Mothers were considerably less likely to help than fathers, and many mothers considered this to be the father's job. This may have been linked to the greater spread of further education

[1] See appendix 4, Table A5.19, p. 237.
[2] See appendix 4, Table A5.20, p. 237.

amongst fathers, much of it of a technical kind, so that they were more able to give the help that was needed. Even so, much of the help given took the form of talking over problems and giving encouragement.

Less help was given with foreign languages, fathers in particular being much less likely to help with languages than with maths. In most cases, however, for both mothers and fathers this help took the form of talking over problems and hearing vocabulary, as few parents had any knowledge of a foreign language. Such help, therefore, even more than in the case of maths homework, may represent parental interest rather than parental skill.

Help with homework was positively related to school achievement ($p = < \cdot 05$) for both maths and languages for fathers, and languages for mothers. In the case of mothers' help with maths the tendency is present but is not significant.

When we turn to look at the pattern of help with homework for the third year extreme groups,[1] which was obtained from interviews during the boys' fourth year at the school, the picture is, however, a very different one. The amount of help with homework is now very much reduced and only a minority of boys now get any help at all from either of their parents. The general impression received from the interviews was that, in all the schools, the level of work had by the fourth year gone beyond the great majority of parents, so that they were unable to give even the minimum of help. Moreover, in the case of mathematics there was very little relationship between help with homework and success, and unsuccesssful boys were almost as likely to receive help as successful boys. In the case of foreign languages the tendency for successful boys to be more likely to receive help is more pronounced and in the case of mothers, when χ^2 was used, was found to be significantly related to success ($p = < \cdot 01$).

The relationship between help with homework and school achievement is therefore a very complex one, and its relationship to the educational level of the parents by no means clear. The findings for the first year extreme groups suggest that, in the early stages of the boy's school career, help with homework

[1] See appendix 4, Table A5.21, p. 238.

may well have been a factor in his success. The consistent tendency for successful boys to have more help than unsuccessful boys is particularly remarkable since it was very obviously the unsuccessful boys who needed help. It will be recalled how frequently the parents of unsuccessful boys reported problems with homework.

By the fourth year, not only were fewer boys receiving help, but, with the exception of mothers' help with languages, this help is not very highly related to achievement. It seems likely, therefore, that it is during the earlier years at secondary school that parental help and encouragement is most important. It is true that, even in the fourth year, mothers' help with languages is still significantly related to success, but since this help mainly took the form of helping with vocabulary, it is probably a measure of the mother's involvement with the boy rather than of the boy's need of help with homework.

Although our findings demonstrate a relationship between help with homework and school achievement, at least in the early years at secondary school, the type of data that we have does not allow us to map out in any detail the manner in which this help is important. There is however reason to suppose, from the parents' own comments, that the great majority were not able to give much practical assistance with specific problems. Very few parents had the knowledge or the technique to do this, and even when the material to be learned was familiar to them, particularly in mathematics, the technique was not. Frequently they were afraid to help in case they muddled the child and made matters worse. In so far as the help they gave was effective, therefore, it seems to have been in an *indirect* rather than a *direct* way. If it did nothing else, it seemed to have underlined in a very concrete way the parents' belief in the importance of homework for success at school. Although some of the parents of unsuccessful boys were well aware of the significance of homework, others readily accepted the excuses of their sons that they had been given no homework for that night, or had done it at school, or on the bus.

In so far as help with homework is an indirect rather than a direct influence on school achievement, the educational level of the parent is of less importance. Many of the mothers who helped with vocabulary, for example, had no knowledge at all of the language involved. On the other hand the parent with experience of private study, either at school or in further education, would be likely to have a greater understanding of the importance of homework, and would be less likely to accept excuses that it had been done at school or on the bus. Such parents, too, might have more confidence in their ability to help. Moreover, in the early years at the school they would have been able to give practical help, as some fathers did with mathematics, even if it got beyond them, as it did with almost all fathers, by the fourth year. Help with homework, therefore, appears to be related both to the educational level of the parent, and the kind of relationship between the parent and the child. We shall return to this point again in a later chapter (see pp. 125–6).

4 CONCLUSION

So far in this chapter we have considered the relationship between several different measures or indices of social class or socio-economic status and school achievement. It remains now to consider how they are related to each other. For this purpose seven of the indices described earlier were selected, father's occupation, father's and mother's secondary education, and further or higher education, family income, and paternal grandfather's occupation. The interrelationship between these seven items was then examined using χ^2. The item on fathers' occupation was related to *all* the other items, and so were the items on income, and both fathers' and mothers' secondary education. On the other hand paternal grandfathers' occupation was not related either to income or to the higher education of either parent. Nor were the items on further or higher education of mothers and fathers related to each other.

The high level of interrelationship between several of these measures suggested the possibility of combining them into a single measure of social or socio-economic status for the purpose of further analysis. It was decided however not to take this step, since it seemed more valuable to examine separately their relationship with other parental variables, particularly child-rearing patterns, and with pupil measures of achievement, motivation, aspirations and personality. Accordingly, fathers' occupation, paternal grandfathers' occupation and fathers' secondary education were all retained as single items. The two items on mothers' education, which were interrelated, were grouped as there seemed no reason to distinguish them.[1] When the scores for mothers' education were compared for the third year extreme groups in all schools, using analysis of variance, the difference between the groups was significant ($F = 4.67$, $p = < .05$).[2] Fathers' further and higher education was however combined not with fathers' secondary education, but with income, because these two items seemed to form a distinctive and closely related group. When these two items were combined and the scores were compared for the third year extreme groups, using analysis of variance, the difference between groups was not significant ($F = 1.73$),[3] although in both the traditional grammar and the comprehensive schools the families of unsuccessful boys had lower scores.

Nevertheless, the scores in this cluster, along with the scores for mothers' education, and the three single items, fathers' occupation, paternal grandfathers' occupation and fathers' secondary education, were all carried forward into the next stage of the analysis. Before proceeding with this further analysis, however, it is necessary to draw together our findings so far and to make some preliminary assessment of the part played by social class in the school achievement of the boys in our particular sample.

We have shown already that, in spite of the homogeneity within schools in respect of socio-economic background, social class as measured by fathers' occupation tended to be related to success in all the three schools, and that within the traditional grammar school this relationship was a very marked one. In the third year extreme groups there were in this school only two 'unsuccessful' boys according to our definition (that is in the extremely unsuccessful group) from non-manual families, and

[1] See appendix 3, p. 205.
[2] See appendix 4, Table A5.22, p. 238.
[3] See appendix 4, Table A5.23, p. 239.

only two 'successful' boys (that is in the extremely successful group) from manual families. In all three schools combined there were only *four* boys from non-manual families in the extremely unsuccessful group. Successful boys with fathers in manual jobs were less rare but, in all three schools combined, there were only thirteen such boys compared with twenty-five working-class boys in the unsuccessful category. Even in the comprehensive school, which was largely working-class in social composition, four out of ten boys in our third year extreme group of successful boys had fathers in non-manual occupation. We will take a closer look at the 'successful' working-class boys in the next chapter.

Turning now to other measures of socio-economic status, or associated indices, the picture is less clearcut. Mothers' occupation, for example, was not found to show any relationship with school achievement for our sample, nor was maternal grandfathers' occupation, although both have been found to be important in other studies. Family size was also found to be largely unrelated to school achievement, and so were family activities and interests, although a very small group of families with what we defined as 'intellectual' interests nearly all had sons in the extremely successful group. Income and other measures of the material environment also showed only a very small relationship to success. Consequently, alongside fathers' occupation we have to set only parental educational background and paternal grandfathers' occupation as having any marked relationship with school achievement for our sample.

Since neither fathers' nor grandfathers' occupation, nor even parental educational background, can in themselves be seen as causal variables, in any attempt to explain the process of school achievement it is necessary now to examine social class background in a wider context, and in particular to see how it relates to the whole process of socialization as well as to aspects of pupil motivation and pupil personality. We take up this task in the following chapter.

CHAPTER SIX

THE PROCESS OF ACHIEVEMENT

I THE FACTORS ASSOCIATED WITH SUCCESS

The first major aim of this study was to identify those characteristics of the pupil and his family which, in the case of this particular sample, appeared to be associated with success. Moreover, without claiming to be in any way exhaustive, variables from a number of different areas and different academic disciplines, which earlier research has shown to be related to success, were included. Previous chapters have dealt in turn with these areas, and examined their relationship to school achievement as defined by our criteria. It is now possible, therefore, to review the characteristics associated with success, and to compile from them a profile of the successful boy and his parents. Before this is done, however, it is necessary to remind the reader of the nature of the sample on which the findings are based.

In the first place it will be recalled that our sample is composed of boys of average and above average ability undergoing academic examination courses in three schools. Although the actual range of ability in the sample was wide, none of the boys was of below average ability. Consequently we are dealing with a selected group, from which it is not possible to generalize about the age group as a whole. Moreover, throughout the study, we are examining the characteristics associated with success or failure in a traditional academic setting. Although there were differences between schools, which we shall explore more fully later, all of the pupils in our sample were following a traditional academic secondary school course with an external examination as its goal.

It is also necessary to bear in mind the limited range of socio-economic background represented in our sample. Not only were there few examples of marked poverty and serious overcrowding, but, more surprisingly, there were also few parents from what we might term a traditional middle-class background. Even those parents classified by the father's occupation as non-manual came, in large measure, from a working-class background themselves. This is reflected in the restricted educational experience of parents in all three schools. Even fathers in a non-manual occupation had not normally attended a selective school. The majority of parents in the random sample were classified on the basis of the interview as occasional or non-readers. Thus we are dealing with a relatively homogeneous group of boys and their families, and this was accentuated by the system of allocation to secondary schools described in an earlier chapter. In any within-school comparison, therefore, the homogeneity of parental background as of the ability level of the boys was very considerable. The failure of some of our variables to relate to success although they have been found to do so very consistently in other studies must be attributed to this high level of homogeneity not only within schools, but to a lesser degree in the sample as a whole.

The definition of success and failure used in this study must also be taken into consideration. The boys in our successful and unsuccessful groups were chosen because their performance in school examinations departed significantly from what might have been expected from their 11-plus scores.[1] They are there-fore those boys who are sometimes referred to as over- and under-achievers. Some boys who were doing badly at school do not come into our sample because such poor performance might have been predicted from their 11-plus score. Similarly, boys doing well did not necessarily fall into our sample if they had

[1] For details of the method employed see appendix 2, pp. 196–8.

E

high 11-plus scores and so were, in our terminology, achieving as expected. Our extreme groups of successful and unsuccessful boys, on which the great bulk of the analysis has been made, were therefore a very specific category, and imply a special and perhaps limited kind of success and failure. On the other hand, in spite of the way in which they were selected, these groups cannot be regarded simply as statistical constructs. The very high relationship between our categories and the parents' perception of the progress at school clearly demonstrates this point. The boys' deterioration or improvement was recorded by the teachers in the school and passed on to the parents by means of school reports, place in the form and promotion or demotion between forms. It would seem therefore that the criterion of success used is meaningful from the point of view of the participants as well as the researchers. Its limitations must, however, be continually borne in mind.

Before going on to review the characteristics associated with success, one further issue arising out of the methods of study must be raised. The decision to make an intensive study of a relatively small group of boys and their parents has meant that the actual number involved, particularly within schools, has been very small. Consequently, for most of the later analysis, the three schools were combined. It is necessary therefore to consider how far this procedure can be justified. For this purpose, the relationship between each variable and success has been examined for each school, using analysis of variance, to determine how far the nature of the relationship was consistent across schools. In almost every case[1] which was carried forward for further analysis, the nature of the relationship was consistent in each of the schools, although the actual strength of the relationship varied, at times, considerably. Hence it was felt that the data could be combined with confidence, and in the remainder of this chapter the findings described relate to the three schools taken together.

As a result of the preliminary analysis of the data described in the previous chapter we were left with twenty-nine factors or

[1] The exceptions were interest in girls, expressed achievement score and active/passive score.

variables, most of these being in the form of clusters or scores, although a few were single items. These factors or variables were then examined in relationship to the third year extreme groups, using Kendall's tau, which is a measure of correlation suitable for non-parametic data. The results of this analysis are given in Table 6.1, listed according to whether they refer to data relating to the pupil, or to his parents. They are arranged in order of the value of tau, with those variables having the highest tau value, that is those correlated most highly with success, being placed first. This order corresponds closely to the degree of confidence in the statistical significance of the relationship which was obtained in earlier analyses using analysis of variance or χ^2.

From this table, the description of the kind of boy who in our study was likely to be successful will be seen to be similar to that presented earlier. It is probable that he will be an introvert, have a dependent relationship with his parents, tend to be orientated towards the future, have his sights set high in relation to examination success, be strongly motivated towards achievement, whether such motivation be assessed explicitly from his declared intentions or implicitly from the existence of an internalized need to excel, intellectually curious, prepared to apply himself to educational tasks set for homework, and, in the two grammar schools only, to have little interest in girls. Phantasy achievement and neuroticism had very little direct relationship with success, and this was also true of the active/passive orientation score.

If we turn now to the parental variables associated with success we find that successful boys are more likely to have fathers, and paternal grandfathers, in non-manual occupations. Parents of such boys are also more likely to have had more education than average and (mothers in particular) tend to give more help with homework. A higher than average level of family income is also an advantage, but not a very great one. There is likely to be a warm and affectionate relationship between the boy and his parents, and control is more likely to take the form of withdrawal of love and approval, rather than the use of physical and material methods of reward and punishment. Such parents, too, tend to have educational aspirations for their son, are approving

Table 6.1 *Variables associated with success*

Parental Variables	Tau Value
Satisfaction with boy's progress at school	0·59
Perception of boy's progress at school	0·58
Father's occupation	0·47
Perception of boy's ability	0·43
Paternal grandfather's occupation	0·40
Approval of boy	0·39
Parental aspirations	0·39
Mother's methods of discipline	0·38
Mother's help with homework	0·37
Parental methods of discipline	0·32
Warmth of parent/child relationship	0·25
Father's method of discipline	0·24
Father's education	0·23
Mother's education	0·21
Material level of home	0·18

Pupil Variables	
Homework orientation	0·52
Intellectual curiosity	0·49
Lack of interest in girls	0·40
Introversion	0·36
Pupil aspirations	0·32
Achievement motivation (n/ach)	0·32
Expressed motivation (v/ach)	0·32
Dependence on parents	0·25
Future/present orientation	0·20
Dependent proneness	0·19
Phantasy achievement	0·05
Neuroticism	0·05
Active/passive orientation	0·01

of his efforts at school, and are not only aware of, but also satisfied with, his progress at school.

Such a profile of the successful boy and his parents, however, does little more than describe the *fact* of a relationship between these characteristics of pupils and parents and success at school. In itself it can do little to explain *how* they relate to school success, or in what way they combine in the *process* of school achievement. If we look, for example, at the pupil variables, the highest tau value is that relating to homework orientation which is a measure, derived from the parents, of the boy's readiness to spend time and trouble on his homework. A boy who does not get down to his homework, and we have seen that many of the unsuccessful boys neglected their homework altogether, is only too likely to fail to achieve in the context of an academic course. This particular measure, therefore, would seem to describe behaviour which is in itself linked directly to achievement, but does not help us to understand why some boys, rather than others, have problems over homework. The second highest tau value is for intellectual curiosity. This is not in itself a measure of behaviour but it is easy to imagine that boys with such curiosity would be more likely to get pleasure from school work, and from the tasks set for homework. Lack of interest in girls gives us the next highest tau value followed closely by the measure of introversion. It is possible that these two measures are linked, since it has been found that introverts, as opposed to extraverts, tend to be more interested in books than people. It has also been suggested that introverts tend to be persistent students, and are more accurate and reliable. Indeed all of these four characteristics would appear to hang together, presenting a picture of the 'natural' student who finds pleasure in his school work, who is not likely to be bored by study, and who is not easily tempted away from his homework by his friends. Indeed it is noteworthy that successful boys were more likely to enjoy spending time alone than were unsuccessful boys.

With the exception of the measure of phantasy achievement, which was not related to success, the aspirational and motivational measures had the same tau value, whether they were derived from projective tests, or from questionnaires. However, as we have suggested earlier, the relationship of these motivational factors with success may be rather more complex than any simple correlational approach can reveal. Instead we have put forward a dynamic model which includes the feedback of information about past success and failure. In the case of successful boys with high drive or achievement motive, a high level of expressed achievement would tend to be consistent with their real situation. If the boys had been unsuccessful, however, the expression on their part of a low level of motivation would seem to serve a defensive function and could be interpreted as an attempt to explain away or rationalize their failure in a situation where achievement had a high value. Unfortunately a similar analysis could not be done for the pupils' aspirations as the data were not available.

None of the other pupil variables was very closely related to success, and the only one which seems to merit closer attention at this stage is the questionnaire measure of dependence on parents. It was suggested earlier that this may be seen as a measure of the boy's conformity to parental wishes. If this is so, it could well be linked to the measure on homework orientation, which was derived from the parents' perception of the boy's behaviour. We shall turn to a further consideration of this possibility later.

If we look now at the parental variables, we find a number of very high tau values, suggesting a close relationship with our success category. However, a closer inspection reveals that, considered as possible *causal* variables, they are less illuminating than they appear at first glance. The two highest tau values are satisfaction with boys' progress at school, and perception of boys' progress at school. Both of these are clearly consequences of school progress, and do not help us to understand why some boys are more successful than others. On the other hand, as we pointed out earlier, the perception that parents have of school progress may influence their perception of the boys' ability which also has a high tau value. Those perceptions are also likely to influence parental aspirations for the boys' progress in the future. Some form of emotive reaction is also likely to be associated with such perceptions in parents who value school achievement. We shall return to this point again later. A number of the variables included as measures of socio-economic status were found to be related to success and of these, father's occupation had the highest tau value. This is perhaps surprising when we take into account the poor discrimination of this variable in both the technical grammar and the comprehensive schools. There was, however, a very strong relationship between success and father's occupation in the grammar school, and the tendency was clearly in the same direction in the other two schools in spite of the small numbers in the non-manual category. The other socio-economic variable with a high tau value is paternal grandfather's occupation. This discriminated slightly less well than father's occupation, but on the other hand it was very rare to find an unsuccessful boy with a paternal grandfather in the non-manual category. Our findings therefore are in line with other research which has established a close link between social class and school achievement, although the *nature* of the link still has to be explored.

When we turn to the measures of parental education we find that they have relatively low tau values and it is clear that, as far as this sample is concerned, the two occupational indices have greater value as predictors of success than either mother's or father's level of education. This finding may reflect the fact that the successful boys appeared, in themselves, to have the basic ingredients that make for academic success in the particular kind of educational setting described in this study, and hence they would require little if any direct help from the parents. With the unsuccessful boys, such help would presumably have been of assistance to them but given the relatively low level of parental education, the earlier comments of the parents suggest that the quality of the direct help would have been poor.

The only other socio-economic measure included in this part of the analysis was the material level of the home, but this finding may well be peculiar to the particular sample of parents with which we are dealing. It is necessary, therefore, to turn to other parental variables for an explanation of the success of the middle-class parents in our study. It should be remembered, however, that the occupational measures probably owe their high correlation with success to the fact that they are indices representing a whole series of parental and environmental attributes, some of which we may have measured inadequately, and some we may not have included at all. We cannot hope, therefore, for any complete explanation.

The other parental variables included in our analysis are those which attempt to measure the nature of the parent/child relationship and the pattern of child-rearing associated with them. As will be seen from Table 6.1, the measure of methods of discipline, particularly those of the mother, had a relatively high tau value, as did the mother's help with homework. Parental approval and pride also had a fairly close relationship with success. The possibility that these are causal variables operating through the personality and motivation of the boy has been explored in an earlier chapter, but we have still to consider how far they can explain the social class differences in school achievement.

It is clear, therefore, that although Table 6.1 allows us to compare the relative predictive power of individual variables, this does not take us very far in in our understanding of the complex process of school achievement. We need to take our analysis a stage further and to examine the interrelationships *among* variables, for patterns of relationships between personality and social structure in particular, if the interdisciplinary nature of our research is to have any real meaning. It is to the search for these interrelationships that we now turn.

2 TOWARDS AN UNDERSTANDING OF SCHOOL ACHIEVEMENT

Although one of the main aims of this research was to discover ways in which the variables related to success are also related to each other, it was realized, from an early stage, that the difficulties in carrying out such an analysis were formidable. Without wishing to go too deeply into the technical issues it is necessary to review them briefly in order to explain the procedure that was finally adopted. One of the most serious problems was the disparate nature of the data that we had collected, ranging as they did from scores based on questionnaire responses on the one hand to interviewers' impressions of family relationships on the other. Another problem arose from the nature of our sample, based as it was on boys falling into the 'extreme' categories of success and failure. The small size of the sample was also a source of difficulty in a number of ways. In the final analysis it became clear to us that no statistical procedure was entirely suited to our problem, since all the techniques we might have used depended for their strict application upon conditions which our data could not fulfil.

On the other hand, we were not concerned in this study primarily with the testing of hypotheses, but with the discovery of *probable* patterns of relationships which could be formulated as hypotheses which, at a later stage, could be submitted to a more rigorous test. We chose therefore to make use of the technique of hierarchical linkage analysis[1] in spite of the problems and doubts associated with its use in a sample such as ours. The purpose of this particular technique is to discover the pattern of relationships among a number of variables by grouping them into a series of 'clusters' in such a manner that each variable is placed beside those other variables to which it is most highly related.

This analysis, the results of which can be represented diagrammatically, as in Fig. 6.1, shows two distinct clusters.[2] Within each of these, the variables are linked together by lines, at different levels, represented by numbers on the vertical axis. The lower the level at which variables or groups of variables link together, the closer the relationship.

If we turn now to look more closely at cluster 1 we see that it is in fact a fairly loose grouping of several smaller clusters, or subclusters. The measures of parents' perception of boys' progress and satisfaction with boys' progress are, for example, in very close linkage, and joined with these at the next level of linkage is parents' perception of the boys' ability. Also linked at this level are the emotional warmth of the home and the parental approval of and pride in the boy. All of these measures or variables link together at level 3, which means that they are more closely related to each other than to any other variable. The measure of the boy's dependence on his parents is also part of this sub-cluster.

The very close relationship between parents' satisfaction with

---

[1] For a description of this technique see appendix 6, pp. 247–8.
[2] In this analysis, the criterion variable of success was omitted.

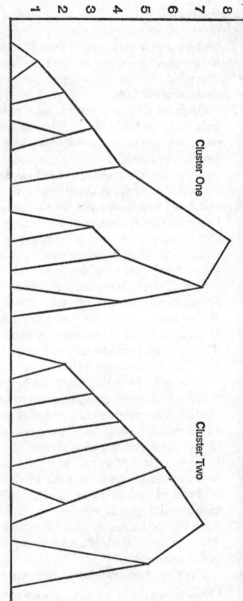

Figure 6.1 *Cluster analysis*

and perception of boys' progress is very probably a reflection of the very high value placed by these parents on success at school. Moreover, as we have seen, the perceptions of these parents were on the whole extremely accurate even when using our own rather complicated definition of achievement. School success, as we have noted earlier, is also taken by the parents as evidence of ability. The close link between these variables and the measures of parental warmth and approval suggest that the nature of the parent/child relationship is, in part at least, conditional upon success. On the other hand, the presence of the measure of dependence on parents in this cluster suggests the possibility of a more complex process in which warm approving parents may tend to produce dependent boys who, in order to maintain a loving relationship, conform to the expectations of their parents. It is these conformist boys, as we have seen, who are likely to be successful at school. To their success their parents react with still more warmth and approval. In such an interpretation, parental warmth and approval can be regarded as both cause and consequence of school success.

A further grouping within cluster 1 shows parental aspirations to be associated with intellectual curiosity at level 3 and both these with homework orientation at level 4. The latter variable was derived from the parental interviews, and is a measure of their perception of the boys' commitment to the homework situation. It is interesting that this should be linked to the measure of intellectual curiosity derived from a questionnaire given to the boys, which suggests that commitment to homework is not simply a measure of conformity but may be influenced to an even greater extent by the boys' interest in intellectual and academic issues. Both, however, appear to be used by parents as guides in the formulation of their educational aspiration for their sons. Finally, in cluster 1, introversion is found linked to lack of interest in girls and at a lower level of relationship with the sub-cluster of parental aspirations, intellectual curiosity and home-work situation. This finding supports various hypotheses about introverts, i.e. that they are less socially aware than extroverts, have more interest in books and intellectual problems and are more able and willing to persist in working at an academic task.

We have, therefore, in cluster 1 a group of variables in which aspects of pupil personality are related to parental perceptions, including aspirations, and the emotional and affective links between parent and child. Of particular interest, however, is the way in which the parental variables in this cluster appear, in large part, to be reactions to, or reflections of, the measures of personality and other *pupil* variables. Even parental aspirations, because of their links with homework orientation, intellectual curiosity and introversion rather than with any of the socio-economic variables, seem more appropriately viewed in this way.

As has been pointed out earlier, parental aspirations in any representative sample of parents are related to social class. What the data of this study demonstrate however is that, given the limitations of our sample, these aspirations are modified and influenced by the perceptions that parents have of the progress and behaviour of their own children to such an extent that any relationships that their aspirations have with other variables are very much closer to their perceptions of their children than they are to any socio-economic factors.

The situation with respect to cluster 2 is very different, how-ever, since all of the social class background factors fall into this cluster, and four of them, the material level of the home, father's education, father's occupation and mother's education form a sub-cluster in which they are more related to each other than to any other item. This goes some way to support the argument that father's occupation is representative of a number of vari-ables including parental education and the material level of the home. At the next level, mother's help with homework is related to this sub-cluster, suggesting that her ability to help, even in the limited form that we found such help to take, is dependent upon her educational level.

The next sub-cluster combines three items on parental disci-pline which, at level 6, are related to the social class sub-cluster. This confirms the view found in the literature that types of punishment or methods of discipline are related to social class or socio-economic background. This sub-cluster is not, however, closely related to any of the pupil variables, and the only measure of personality to fall within cluster 2 is the measure of need

for achievement, which is related to paternal grandfather's occupation at level 5 and to the other variables in this cluster at level
7. At the present stage of the analysis it is difficult to suggest any
explanation why this should be so, or why paternal grandfather's
occupation should be more closely related to need for achievement than are the immediate parental social class variables.
Chance factors in the small samples employed in this study may
well be responsible. On the other hand there is support in the
literature for the finding that need for achievement measures are
related both to socio-economic status and to methods of parental
discipline.

Apart from these two clusters, the remainder of the variables
did not appear to be related either to each other or to the other
clusters. The exception to this was neuroticism and phantasy
achievement which formed a reciprocal pair related at level 6.
It is important to remember that neither of these variables is
related to success. Hence, the tendency for neurotic boys to
engage in phantasy achievement is not a consequence of their
failure to achieve. In other words neurotic boys, regardless of
the degree of their success, tend to engage in phantasy achievement. It is interesting to note that neuroticism is not related to
actual educational aspirations and expectations and hence,
although highly neurotic children have high phantasy achievement, this does not carry over into real-life aspirations.

Boys' aspirations and expectations did not form part of the
cluster which included parental aspiration. On the other hand
when a measure of boys' perception of parental aspiration was
included in the cluster analysis it formed a reciprocal pair with
the boys' own aspirations. This suggests that the boys' perceptions of their parents' aspirations are influenced more by their
own aspirations than by their parents'.

The measures of achievement orientation included in the
study, namely active/passive orientation, future/present orientation and achievement values or expressed motivation were all
found to be unrelated either to each other or to any of the
clusters. Possible reasons for this will be discussed in the context
of 'the achievement syndrome'.

3 THE ACHIEVEMENT SYNDROME

The pattern of interrelationships which has emerged from the hierarchical analysis has various points of similarity with the position taken up by Rosen[1] and by Rosen and d'Andrade[2] and also important points of difference. As early as 1956 Rosen introduced the concept of the achievement syndrome which includes on the one hand a psychological factor of achievement motivation or need for achievement, and on the other certain educational and occupational aspirations and a number of value orientations which define, for the individual, behaviour appropriate to the implementation of achievement motivation. Rosen argued that his two concepts of the achievement syndrome differed in their origins.

He maintained that achievement motivation was probably associated with certain kinds of parent/child interaction. The nature of these he investigated with d'Andrade in a study which was important methodologically because it did not depend on interview data but was based on observation of ongoing parent/child behaviour. In that study the authors found that parents of boys with high achievement scores had high parental aspirations for them to do well at any given task, combined with a high regard for their competence. Moreover, as they progressed, parents tended to react to their performance with warmth and approval or, in the case of mothers especially, with disapproval of a poor performance. Fathers of these boys were willing to take a back seat while their sons were performing but the mothers tended to become emotionally involved. Indeed the authors argue that high maternal involvement is the major factor differentiating between high and low need for achievement. Rejecting and dominating fathers are associated with low need for achievement, it is suggested, because they are perceived as threatening. The findings of the present study are very much in

[1] B. C. Rosen, 'The achievement syndrome: a psychocultural dimension of social stratification', *American Sociological Review*, XX (1956), pp. 155–61.
[2] B. C. Rosen and R. d'Andrade, 'The psychosocial origins of achievement motivation', *Sociometry*, XXII (1959), pp. 183–218.

line with those of Rosen and d'Andrade as is demonstrated by the association of love-oriented discipline, maternal involvement with homework and high need for achievement in our second cluster which shows all of these to be relative to socioeconomic factors. This would seem to suggest the possibility that one reason for the greater success of our middle-class or non-manual sample was the use by their parents of a pattern of discipline which favoured the development of a high need for achievement.

In cluster 1, parental warmth and approval was associated with parental perception of and satisfaction with success at school, and we have noted earlier the relationships between hostile rejecting fathers and failure. This leads us to propose a dynamic model in which the lack of success at school is perceived by the parents and reinforces their rejection, just as the warmth and approval of the parents of successful boys is influenced by their perception of the boys' success. It would seem that a 'feedback' model of this kind is more appropriate to the conceptualization of school achievement than an oversimplistic view which has, as its main characteristic, sociological determinism.

The origins of achievement orientation are less clearly set out by Rosen, although the assumption seems to be that they are transmitted perhaps at the verbal level from parent to child. Taking aspirations first, our data showed that parental aspirations and parental perceptions of the boys' ability were also included in cluster 1. These particular variables, however, were associated in our analysis with neither the pupils' need for achievement nor socio-economic factors. Instead, we found them to be related to such aspects of the pupils' personality as introversion and lack of interest in girls, homework orientation, intellectual curiosity and dependence on adults. Although we have always to bear in mind the limitations of our data, and particularly our sample, it would appear that these personality variables need to be explored more fully in their relationship to the achievement syndrome.

From the data at present available, however, it appears that aspirations should be regarded as part of a dynamic process which allows for the modification of the aspirations and expectations of both pupils and parents in the light of the experience of the boy in school. Although there is evidence that the great majority of parents placed a high instrumental value on success at school, the extent to which this was perceived as a personal goal depended on a number of factors, including the perceived ability of the boy, his apparent motivation to succeed and his own aspirations for the future.

Pupil aspirations, however, were not found to be related to either of the major clusters and clearly much more work is needed to explore what is clearly a complex set of relationships. But it can perhaps be argued that a case has been made out for a dynamic rather than a static approach to both aspirations and values, and their relationship to both school achievement and social class.

With regard to value orientations,[1] Rosen used questionnaires based on Kluckhohn's value orientations to compare the values of mothers and their sons. He found that mothers whose values were similar to those of their sons, irrespective of the direction of these values, were more likely to report the use of love-oriented techniques such as displays of affection, reasoning and appeals to standards.

In our study the boys' value orientations as measured by questionnaire responses did not relate very strongly to school achievement. Nor in the final analysis were they found in association with any of the measures of discipline, or with parent/child relationships. We were not therefore able to tie high value orientation to any particular aspect of parental behaviour or home background. On the other hand the association in cluster 1, between parental warmth and approval and conformity to parental standards, is at least in part in line with Rosen's findings with respect to the internalization of parental standards.

Several reasons can be advanced for the absence of relationships demonstrated in relation to the boys' value orientations. One is that, at the level of individuals, such orientations can be regarded as a set of beliefs about the self in relation to the

[1] B. C. Rosen, 'Family structure and value transmission', *Merrill-Palmer Quarterly*, X (1964).

environment, the future and other people.[1] Hence questionnaires may be inappropriate measures of these beliefs. Pupils' awareness of the kind of beliefs they are expected by parents and teachers to have about these matters, rather than what they actually believe, may be what the questionnaires are measuring. Another reason may be that the nature of the relationships associated with these beliefs may be very complex. As was the case with expressed achievement, the pupils' beliefs or expressions of beliefs could serve both predictive and defensive functions for them,[2] and more sophisticated research designs than were possible in this study may be necessary to untangle the complexities of those relationships.

4 SUCCESSFUL WORKING-CLASS BOYS

The hierarchical analysis has demonstrated a relationship between social class background, patterns of child-rearing and the development of high motivation to achieve on the part of the child – a causal sequence which might go some way to explain the higher level of achievement of middle-class children or, more precisely, children from non-manual families. Successful working-class children, it could then be hypothesized, would tend to come from homes where the techniques of child-rearing approximated to those of the middle class.

While it would have been valuable to test this hypothesis statistically – and even more desirable to do separate analyses for successful working-class and middle-class, and unsuccessful working-class and middle-class groups separately – this was not possible with the small numbers available in our sample. Instead we have used the interviews to do a descriptive analysis in order to highlight features in the home background of the working-class boys which might seem to explain their success. Since the definition of school achievement, or 'over-achievement', used so far in this study is based on a comparison within schools, it seems most useful at least initially to make the analysis school by school.

[1] See chapter 3.
[2] M. B. Smith, J. S. Bruner and R. W. White, *Opinions and Personality* (New York, Wiley, 1956).

There were only two successful working-class boys in the third year extreme groups at the traditional grammar school, in comparison with seven working-class boys who were unsuccessful. It is therefore worth looking at these two rather unusual boys in some detail. Thomas Ellis's father was in a semi-skilled job although he had started out as a skilled craftsman. His mother's occupation was also in the manual category, and so were both grandparents. Neither parent had any education other than in an ordinary elementary school, and neither had any hobbies or interests of an 'intellectual' kind, although the father was a shop steward. There were two younger sisters and the family lived in a council house. So far, therefore, there is nothing remarkable in the family background of this boy, and certainly nothing to explain his success, since it is in no way different from those of the working class who were in our unsuccessful group.

If however we turn to the child-rearing techniques and, in particular, to the emotional background of the home, a very different picture is presented. These parents made little use of what we have called the physical or material type of punishment, and, although they occasionally deprived him of sweets, etc., they said that he was 'too sensitive to smack'. In order to encourage him they used praise, and also example. The father told the interviewer that he would 'tell him of the chances I've missed'. There was never any problem over homework or indeed any other aspect of behaviour, and the parents were 'proud of everything'. They saw his good behaviour as a sign of his affection for them, and of his good sense. To the question on trouble over friends they replied that they were confident of his ability not to be easily led. When they were asked about the help they could give him they replied, 'He is streets ahead of us.' The interviewer commented on this family, 'This boy seems to be surrounded by an aura of pride, affection and almost wonder.'

The second boy, Norman Stokes, had a father in semi-skilled manual work and a mother who had been in domestic service. Her father, however, had had a small shop, so that she fell into the category that Jackson and Marsden call 'sunken middle class'. Neither parent, however, had had anything other than an ordinary elementary school education. There were five other children, and the family lived in a rented house. Norman was the first child in the family to 'pass' the 11-plus and his older brothers and sisters had been to secondary modern schools. Apart from the maternal grandfather, therefore, there was nothing to distinguish this family from others in the working class.

Like Thomas Ellis, however, Norman had been given considerable encouragement by his parents to do well at school. His father told him, 'don't end up in an uninteresting job like me', and urged him to 'do more with his life than I have'. They had bought him a lot of books, often at financial sacrifice, including a set of encyclopedias on hire purchase which Norman used for his homework. Like Thomas, too, Norman received nothing but praise from his parents throughout the interview. 'He's perfect', they said, and praised him not only for his school achievement but for his good behaviour, consideration and honesty. Also, like Thomas's parents, they used a minimum of physical and material punishment, and indeed scarcely needed to use any control at all. This was partly because of their tolerance; when he grew his hair long they didn't interfere, and they approved of him putting his own point of view, but partly also because of their confidence in his maturity. For example, they let him select his own programme on television, since his choice was more 'highbrow' than their own. 'He has always been ahead of us', they said.

Within the group of seven unsuccessful working-class boys there were several parents whose social class background and educational experience might have led us to expect that their children would be successful at grammar school. One boy's father was a foreman who had been to a selective secondary school until he was fifteen and had afterwards acquired a minor qualification by part-time study. His mother, who had been in clerical work before marriage, was a keen reader. Another boy, whose father had followed a course of further part-time education, had a mother who had been to a selective secondary school until she was fifteen, and had worked as a clerk. Three other mothers had been in a clerical occupation before marriage and another was 'sunken-middle-class'. In fact, however, these aspects of parental background and educational experience seem to have been less important than the relationships within the family in differentiating between successful and unsuccessful boys. The atmosphere of affection and pride which was so characteristic of the families of the two successful boys is largely absent when we turn to look at the unsuccessful working-class boys in this school.

The greatest contrast is provided by the boy, already described in an earlier chapter, whose relationship with his father appeared to be one of unrelieved hostility and rejection. Punishment, particularly, from the father was very harsh and included beatings, as distinct from the smack or 'thump' found in most families when physical punishment was used. There was also a considerable amount of material deprivation which took severe and unusual forms. For example on several occasions the boy was deprived of meals as a punishment. It was in this family, too, that the rather bizarre incident occurred where the boy was made to eat two cigarettes when he was discovered smoking. Although relationships were better with the mother, who would take her son's part in some of their quarrels, she appeared to give him very little praise or approval. Moreover, although the father accused her of being too soft, and she did not seem to smack the boy, she was very critical of his behaviour and seemed to nag him continually. The pressure to achieve at school was very strong from both parents and the boy's failure to do well was a central focus of rows, but this was only one aspect of a whole range of discipline problems, including lying, disobedience and cheekiness as well as hair, TV and friends.

In no other family had relationships deteriorated to this extent. Nevertheless, even within this small group of seven boys there was one other case of apparent rejection by the father, and the use of a considerable amount of physical punishment. Although both parents admired their son's intelligence, they criticized him constantly throughout the interview, calling him selfish, obstinate and 'too mature and aloof'. The mother shouted and nagged a great deal and used the cane regularly, and although the father did not cane or smack, he used material deprivation a great deal, and, in his own words, 'showed contempt'. It was not altogether clear what these punishments were for, although there was trouble over hair, and homework was described as 'a constant worry'.

Although this kind of relationship was rare, there were several cases of families where, in spite of evidence of some warmth and affection and a willingness to give praise, there was also a heavy reliance on physical or material deprivation. The parents of one boy, for example, were clearly very closely involved with their only son and praised him warmly, particularly for his generous and outgoing nature. They said of him, 'he's grown the way we want him to be'. The major source of dissension was the boy's lack of progress at school, and the fact that he did not seem to try to do better. Homework was a permanent battleground although by the fourth year they had to a large extent given up trying, and accepted the situation. There was also trouble over friends, since his parents did not like his friends and thought he was easily led. TV was another source of tension. The technique of control used was also exclusively smacking and material deprivation. They often, for example, deprived him of his pocket money as a punishment or turned off the television. Nagging at him, shouting and the use of threats were also used a great deal, particularly the threat to make him leave school. This had the power to upset him but not to make him take more pains over his homework. Indeed none of the punishment used seemed to have much effect. Thus, though these parents praised the boy's personality, they punished much of his behaviour and particularly that which reflected his lack of progress in school.

In another family where a close and affectionate relationship was combined with some physical punishment and where the use of material deprivation was the major technique of discipline, there was little or no pressure exerted upon the boy to succeed. This lack of achievement was blamed largely on the school and his attempts to evade homework were treated half humorously. For example, the father, who took a major role in the interview and seemed to be the more important parent in the boy's upbringing, treated as a joke the boy's practice of doing his homework on the bus.

The absence of any strong parental pressure to succeed was a characteristic of one other case in the unsuccessful group. This boy came from a large family and was living in considerable poverty due to the chronic ill-health of the father. The family had lived until very recently in a flat in one of the worst of the city slums, and the possible effect of this on the children was a recurrent theme throughout the interview. Perhaps because of their difficult circumstances and the large number of siblings there was little emotional involvement with the boy on the part of the parents, who tended to leave him to sort out his own problems. They had little knowledge of how he was doing at school and showed little interest in his progress. Indeed their main anxiety was to keep him out of trouble with the police, and to this end they had in previous years, while living in the flat, exercised close control over his friends. They could not therefore be described as neglectful parents, but their aspirations had been limited by their exceptional environment. Most of the criticism was centred on the boy's temper, and his insistence on getting his own way, and not at all on homework, which did not really concern them. Smacking, threats and material deprivation had been the major techniques of control, although smacking was no longer used by either parent now that the boy was older.

The remaining two working-class families in the unsuccessful groups used a mixture of disciplinary techniques in which love-oriented methods played some part. In one case the parents made use of a variety of methods, including coaxing, and reasoning or explanation. On the other hand there had been a lot of smacking in the past, and it had been dropped only because 'it doesn't work now'. Other methods used including keeping in, sending to bed and, in the father's own words, 'showing I dislike him'. Of all the methods, the parents thought that 'keeping in works best'. There were problems over answering back, and the boy was described as noisy and cheeky. Homework was a focus of rows and there was quite a lot of pressure from the parents for success at school. In the other case, although the parents had occasionally smacked their son and sometimes shouted at him, reasoning was the most usual method of discipline. The parents said that they tried to make him see the consequences of his actions and when they caught him smoking, for example, they did not punish him, but tried to explain why he should not smoke. There were problems over homework, over hair and staying out late, but the parents were not highly critical and they praised him for his generosity and lack of jealousy. On the other hand there was considerable pressure to succeed and the parents had paid several visits to the school over his lack of progress.

It is clear therefore that although the unsuccessful working-class families are not all of one type and indeed to a large extent each has quite unique characteristics, there is a pattern in the parental responses which tends to differentiate unsuccessful from successful boys. Moreover these differences appear to lie in the family/child relationships, particularly in the disciplinary techniques, and not in the social origin or educational background of the parents. Pressure to achieve, although absent in two of the unsuccessful families, is clearly present to a high degree in the other five.

Before attempting even the most tentative of generalizations, the number of case studies is so small that it is necessary to examine the working-class boys in the other two schools where working-class success was less rare, before any attempt is made to explore the implications of our findings. There were five successful working-class boys in the third year extreme group at the technical grammar school, compared with nine who were in the extreme unsuccessful group. Of these five boys, three were the sons of foremen or supervisors, and, of the other two boys, one had a mother who was 'sunken-middle-class' since her father had had a small business. The father of the other successful boy had also had, at one time, a business of his own but had gone bankrupt and at the time of the interviews was in a skilled manual occupation. Within the group of nine unsuccessful working-class boys only one was a foreman and only one boy had a parent who was sunken-middle-class. Mothers in non-manual occupation before marriage were, however, found more frequently in the *unsuccessful* group.

Although successful working-class boys were therefore

differentiated to some extent in their social class background from unsuccessful working-class boys, this was not reflected in their parents' educational background, or hobbies and interests. Only a handful of parents had had more than an ordinary elementary education and these were found equally in the unsuccessful and the successful groups. The most educated parents had both had some further part-time education leading to minor qualifications and the mother had won a scholarship and attended a grammar school. These parents were the only two who did any more than very occasional reading. Their son, however, was one of the extremely unsuccessful boys.

It is when we turn to the emotional atmosphere of the home and the technique of discipline and control that we find the most marked differences between the two groups of boys. Of the five parents of the successful boys, three appeared to rely exclusively or mainly on 'love-oriented' methods of control, and of one boy the interviewer reported that he was 'surrounded by powerful parental love, pride and approval'. The father, according to his reports, had never smacked, and the interviewer described him as 'gentle and understanding'. The mother had smacked him when he was young so as not to spoil him, since he was an only child, and now has to shout at him 'occasionally' when he is rude. This boy appears to be obedient and well behaved, although the parents report occasional problems with homework. A second boy seems to have had an equally close and affectionate relationship with his parents, particularly with his father, who seemed to be very closely involved with his son. These parents found nothing to criticize and praised his 'wonderful disposition'. Both parents claimed never to have hit him, in spite of the occasional threat to do so. In fact they were at pains to emphasize the boy's extreme sensitivity even to minor criticisms. 'If you shout at him,' they said, 'he'll cry.' In the case of the third boy in this group there was also evidence of a close affectionate relationship with the parents and considerable praise combined with very little criticism. They were very interested and involved in his school work and spent a lot of time helping, so far as they were able, with his homework. There were very few discipline problems, and they said of him, 'he's only got to be told once', although his father had smacked him occasionally for answering back.

In the case of the other two boys the pattern of relationships is of a more ambiguous kind. For example, there was considerable pride in one of the boys both for his intelligence and his sporting prowess, and evidence of a close relationship with the father in the past, when they had gone together to football matches. The parents reported that when the boy was younger they had read to him 'endlessly'. On the other hand smacking was fairly frequent when he was a small boy. Later the parents and particularly the mother would use the boy's affection for her as a means of control, and in her own words would 'tell him he doesn't love me', or 'tell him I will cry'. The only discipline problem, however, was answering back, which was a focus of rows in the family. The last of the successful boys most nearly approaches middle-class status, since his father, as mentioned earlier, had lost his business through bankruptcy and his mother before marriage had managed a shop. In addition she taught in a Sunday school. Within the family, however, the emotional climate was cold rather than warm. The interviewer described them as cool, inarticulate parents and the father himself admitted that he had left most of the upbringing to the mother. Both parents believed in discouraging the boy from asking for help. Although there had been few discipline problems in the past, the parents reported that in his fourth year at school they were less satisfied with his progress and behaviour. He was slapped 'a good deal lately' mainly for getting on his mother's nerves. This boy is therefore a fairly marked exception to the general relationship between emotional warmth and success at school.

If we turn now to the unsuccessful working-class boys the picture is dramatically different. None of the parents of these boys could be classified clearly and unambiguously as using love-oriented techniques of discipline, and several of them made use of smacking, shouting and material deprivation consistently and frequently. In one such case the father regularly hit his son and had done so since the boy was small. The father, who was described by the interviewer as having an unhappy relationship with his son, also ignored the boy as a punishment, or compared him unfavourably with his brothers and sisters. The mother too used smacking as a discipline technique. There was little praise and a good deal of criticism of this boy, the major source of argument being his lack of success. These parents were the most highly educated of the working-class sample at this school, and were deeply distressed at their son's failure to do well.

Although perhaps this was the extreme case of a rejecting father there were two other boys whose parents used smacking fairly frequently, combined with threats and shouts. One such father said he smacked more now than in the past and also kept the boy in as a punishment. There was a lot of criticism and little praise for this boy, and the father was described by the interviewer as very resentful and annoyed, and complained that the boy 'will ask but won't listen'. Problems were reported not only over homework, staying out late and answering back but also over truancy, lies and pilfering. Yet another boy who received little praise was described by his father as 'too much under your feet'. Discipline was maintained by a lot of smacking and by the use of material deprivation. There was no pressure on the boy to do well, and on homework the father said, 'it's his fault if he doesn't do it'. This was the only family which seemed to have no interest in educational achievement.

No other family in this group showed this combination of harsh punishment and rejection, but all of them used material deprivation, 'telling off' and some smacking as the main form of control. For example, the parents of one boy relied on 'shouting' and material deprivation since they had found that it did no good to hit him. This boy was particularly unhappy at school both in his relationships with teachers and other boys, and truanted several times. They had trouble to get him to do his homework and also over friends. In another case, although the father never smacked, the mother did so occasionally, and he had been hit over his poor school work. In yet another case smacking was used rarely but the boy was continuously criticized for both his behaviour and his poor school work, and homework was a focus of rows. The father also compared him to his detriment with other boys.

As in the traditional grammar school, the successful and unsuccessful working class are therefore quite sharply differentiated in terms of techniques of discipline. Parents of successful boys were also more approving and in general, although certainly not in every case, more affectionate and loving. Almost all the unsuccessful boys in both schools showed a wide variety of discipline problems, covering many aspects of behaviour. As in the traditional grammar school many, although not all, of the unsuccessful parents were very anxious for their child to succeed and placed a lot of emphasis on homework, so that again this does not by itself appear to have been important as an explanation of failure. The only real difference between the two schools is the tendency within the technical grammar school for successful boys to be more likely to have a father who was a foreman. On the other hand educational background, as in the traditional grammar school, was not related to success.

Turning finally to the comprehensive school, there were in the third year extreme groups six successful working-class boys, and nine who were unsuccessful. As we have seen, this school was predominantly working-class in social class composition and in our third year extreme groups there were only four boys from non-manual families and all of these were in the successful group. Both the successful and unsuccessful working-class groups had two boys who were the sons of foremen. There were however four unsuccessful boys with one parent who was 'sunken-middle-class' but no successful boys. Mothers of unsuccessful boys were also more likely to have followed a non-manual occupation. Among successful boys there were two families with more than the minimum educational qualification compared with two families of unsuccessful boys. Neither in social origin nor in educational background therefore did the successful boys have a clear advantage.

Looking however at emotional relationships within the family we find that the majority of successful boys appeared to have close and affectionate relationships with their parents, who used predominantly love-oriented techniques of discipline. Four out of the six parents used approval and praise and what they called 'coaxing' rather than punishment, with the occasional smack often for cheekiness. Of the other two, one smacked quite a lot and the other used mainly threats and material deprivation, although smacking had been used when the boy was younger. None of the parents were highly critical of their sons but they seemed to be less satisfied overall than the parents of successful boys at the two grammar schools. There was criticism for example of cheekiness, temper and untidiness. Television was a source of difficulty in three families when it interfered with homework. In every case, however, parents were very much involved in the boy's success at school, helping with homework as far as they were able, trying to control the time spent on homework and giving plenty of encouragement. In one family, for example, the parents gave a lot of help with homework and although they admitted smacking a lot they said it was never in cold blood. They used a lot of praise and few criticisms and were very proud of the success the boy had had. Another boy had parents who used approval, praise and reasoning although they had smacked occasionally when he was small. There was some criticism of the boy for untidiness and stubbornness, but a lot of praise was also given. In only one case did the pattern of responses approach that typical of the unsuccessful boy. This boy had a father who was a foreman, with some further part-time education leading to a minor qualification. These parents had been disappointed in the boy's 11-plus results, since they would have preferred a grammar school. They said he was 'too big to smack now' but they threatened him and deprived him of things he liked. There had been trouble over hair and TV and, in his fourth year, some problems with homework.

Of the nine unsuccessful boys, the parents of five used fairly frequent smacking combined with material deprivation as the main method of control. The parents of one boy smacked, threatened, shouted, nagged and stopped pocket money. Of these, stopping pocket money was in their opinion the most effective, and this technique was used frequently. This boy was punished for answering back, and for staying out late and also for his poor reports from school. Another boy was also smacked, sent to bed, his pocket money was stopped and he was kept in. His parents were very critical and complained of his staying out late, untidiness, cheek and his attitude to homework. All of these were the focus of family rows. Two other parents no longer smacked, although both had done so in the past, but used threats and material deprivation in one form or another. Of the two remaining boys, one was a child with a record of poor health who was never actually punished. Nevertheless there was a lot of criticism of this boy because of his poor school performance, and the father in particular expressed his disappointment very forcibly throughout the interview. The final boy, however, approximated in his family relationships more closely to the successful than to the unsuccessful group. His parents made few criticisms of the boy and expressed a lot of pride and affection. They did not smack although they occasionally threatened to do so, and used praise and reasoning as their main method of control. There was no indication that they had any discipline problems and although they were aware of the boy's lack of progress at school, they did not seem to make it a focus of rows. Nevertheless they were anxious for him to succeed, helped him as far as they were able with his homework and tried to encourage him to spend more time on his school work. The boy himself was very enthusiastic about athletics at which he worked very hard, and his parents believed that this had interfered with his school work.

On the whole, therefore, the pattern of parent/child relationships at the comprehensive school shows differences between successful and unsuccessful working-class boys very similar to the parent/child relationships at the two grammar schools. Although there were some exceptions, love-oriented techniques of discipline were characteristic of the families of successful rather than unsuccessful boys, and there was more affection and pride and less criticism. Successful boys also seem with certain exceptions to have been more ready to accept parental values and expectations. On the other hand, parents of unsuccessful boys at this school were more likely than those in either of the grammar schools to give little or no encouragement to the boy to succeed. Altogether three of the nine unsuccessful working-class boys had parents who showed in various ways a lack of concern with school achievement, making no attempt for example to control the amount of time or effort the boy gave to his homework, or to persuade or force him to take his work more seriously. Two other parents, although concerned at the boy's lack of progress, made only rather inconsistent attempts at control. In the two grammar schools, in contrast, there were only two families, one in each school, who did not show concern at the boy's lack of progress and take steps to improve his performance, although in one family with a son at the traditional grammar school the pressure seems to have been somewhat halfhearted. Only at the comprehensive school therefore can lack of parental encouragement have played more than a very small part in the lack of progress of the unsuccessful group as a whole.

5 CONCLUSION

Before attempting to draw any conclusions with respect to these findings it is well to emphasize once again the limitations which arise from both the size of the sample and its nature. Although we have made some use throughout of information derived from all the boys, and from a random sample of parents, the hierarchical analysis and the case studies are based on the small groups of extremely successful and unsuccessful boys in each of the three schools. These groups, it will be remembered, are essentially 'over' and 'under' achievers. Further limitation is imposed by the manner in which the data were collected. All the material on techniques of discipline and on the emotional climate of the home is based, ultimately, on the reports by parents of their feelings and behaviour. Although many of them did seem to talk very frankly and freely to the interviewer, and although the manner and style of the interview was designed to avoid superficial or 'conventional' answers, we do not in fact have any real check on what we were told, particularly in the highly sensitive area of techniques of discipline. On the other hand, there is no doubt that within these limitations certain very clear patterns of differences emerged and the findings from the hierarchical analysis which were followed up were certainly confirmed by the case study material relating to the working-class boys.

In the hierarchical analysis the items or measures earlier found to be related to success tended, with certain exceptions, to fall into two main clusters. In the first of these, the emotional climate of the family, parental approval and satisfaction with perceived progress, and parental aspirations were found to be interrelated with certain measures of pupil personality and motivation. These included dependence on adults, intellectual curiosity, homework orientation and introversion.

The second cluster included a number of measures of parental social class background and educational experience, techniques of discipline and the boy's measure of need for achievement or achievement motivation. This clustering of items suggests the possibility not only that love-oriented techniques of discipline are a factor in school achievement in so far as they influence pupil motivation, but also that the differences in school achievement between the social classes are related to the differences between them in patterns of child-rearing. In order to explore this hypothesis further we examined the family background of the successful working-class boys, comparing them in detail with the working-class families whose sons were in the extremely unsuccessful group. The result of this comparison, described in detail in the previous section, confirms the relationship between love-oriented discipline and success *within* the working classes. Although there are some exceptions in each school, in general the pattern of responses with respect to disciplinary techniques was strikingly different in the successful and in the unsuccessful groups. It was not simply that parents of unsuccessful boys smacked more, although they did, but rather that they followed a pattern of discipline in which smacking was combined with material deprivation, shouting, nagging and telling off. Although parents of successful boys occasionally smacked, it was very rare for them to use this particular combination of techniques. Parents of successful boys also tended to have a warmer, more approving and less critical relationship than parents whose sons were in the unsuccessful group. Where the parents of an unsuccessful boy had a close and affectionate relationship it was often combined with smacking, shouting and material deprivation rather than with love-oriented techniques of discipline.

Another feature which emerged very clearly from the case studies was the extent to which successful boys *appeared* to have accepted parental standards and expectations. Some of the parents had no fault to find at all with their sons; others were critical only of minor aspects of behaviour. On the other hand unsuccessful boys, with few exceptions, were a problem to their parents over a very wide range of behaviour. It is possible, of course, that part of this difference can be explained by the operation of some kind of 'halo effect'. Where there was in general a warm and loving relationship, parents might well over-look or minimize behaviour like cheekiness or answering back which would be resented, sometimes deeply, by parents who already disapproved of their son's behaviour. It is unlikely, how-ever, that this can explain away the differences we found.

Of considerable importance was the finding that parent/child relationships and techniques of discipline were more important in differentiating between successful and unsuccessful working-class parents than factors of a socio-economic nature. Only in the grammar technical did we find father's occupational status within the working class, and to a lesser extent social origin, related to success. Even more surprising was the way in which parental educational experience was quite unrelated to success in all three schools. In the hierarchical analysis, as we have seen, parental educational background was related to social class as measured by father's occupation. Father's education and mother's education were also both related to success, although the tau value was not a high one. These relationships however arose because middle-class fathers, or those in non-manual occupations, were both more highly educated and more likely to have sons in the successful group. Within the working class, as we have seen, educational background made no difference, at least as far as our sample is concerned. A further consequence of this finding is that it is not possible to explain the use by some working-class parents of love-oriented techniques of discipline in terms of differences in educational experience.

One further issue highlighted by the case studies is the part played by parental pressure on the boy to succeed. The parents of successful boys, with few exceptions, encouraged school achievement and were deeply involved in the progress of their sons at school. It might seem therefore that parental pressure to achieve was an important factor in their son's success. Yet, as we have seen, the majority of parents of unsuccessful boys were also deeply and emotionally involved in their son's lack of progress. Homework was a focus of rows in many homes and some unsuccessful boys were punished severely for their poor school reports and bad homework marks. Only in the comprehensive school was there more than a small minority of parents who were not interested in school achievement and did not encourage their child to succeed. Moreover, even within the comprehensive school some of the unsuccessful boys had parents who appeared to be very anxious about their son's lack of success, and homework was a source of anxiety and concern. Clearly, therefore, parental pressure or encouragement is not by itself enough, although its absence may well be an important element in progress at school.

It seems possible to go beyond this position and to maintain that parental pressure on a boy to succeed, unless it is exercised in an atmosphere of love and warmth which presupposes sensitivity on the part of the parents to the individuality of their son, seems more likely to be associated with conflict within the family and with failure than with success at school. Thus, if our findings are to be relied on, it is not the fact of parental pressure that is important but the manner in which it is exercised and the nature of the parental encouragement and control employed in relation to it.

CHAPTER SEVEN

THE EFFECT OF THE SCHOOL

I INTRODUCTION

In studies of school achievement both sociologists and psychologists have devoted considerably more attention to the background of the home than to factors within the school itself. Himmelweit and Swift, for example,[1] comment that although the school is also an active socializing agency only the home is studied in the necessary depth. They argue that 'few measures have been developed for understanding how, why, and with what effect the school seeks to influence behaviour and outlook'. Not only has the study of the school been neglected, but also it has been suggested that its influence, in comparison with the home, is less important. This was the conclusion, for example, of the Plowden Report on the achievement of primary school children[2] and of Coleman's investigation of education in the United States.[3] In both cases, however, the school factors

[1] H. T. Himmelweit and B. Swift, 'A model for the understanding of school as a socializing agent', in P. Mussen *et al* (eds.), *Trends and Issues in Developmental Psychology* (New York, Holt, Rinehart and Winston, 1969).

[2] Plowden Report, Report of the Central Advisory Council for Education (England), *Children and their Primary Schools* (London, HMSO, 1967).

[3] J. S. Coleman *et al*, *Equality of Educational Opportunity* (USOE, GPO, 1966).

included were of a limited kind, and weighted towards physical resources in the case of Coleman, and demographic factors like school size in the case of Plowden. In contrast, the longitudinal study carried out by Douglas showed that very good schools, i.e. schools with good examination results, may offset the effects of a bad home, and that bad schools can have harmful effects, particularly on children of moderate ability from working-class homes[1].

The most systematic attempt in this country to examine the interplay between home and school is however the longitudinal study carried out by Himmelweit and her associates between 1952 and 1963.[2] In an attempt to study the effect of different schools on boys from comparable social backgrounds and the effect of the same school on boys of different backgrounds, they studied the third forms of four grammar and five secondary modern schools. Three different types of neighbourhood were represented in the study, a primarily working-class neighbourhood, a mixed neighbourhood and one which was predominantly middle-class. They found that the type of school attended was a better predictor of the behaviour, outlook, values and attainment of the pupil than either his ability or his social background. A follow-up eleven years later served to confirm these earlier findings. The subsequent occupational history, job level, aspiration, and evaluation of his own career depended on the school attended rather than the family background. Although in both grammar and secondary modern schools boys of middle-class background did better than those of working-class background, such differences were small compared to the very large differences between the occupational attainment of boys going to different types of school. Thus the findings of Himmelweit and her associates, taken together with those of Douglas and his team, suggest that the school is, or can be, a factor of some importance in influencing school achievement, and that selection for a grammar school in particular can have a very powerful effect on future occupational achievement.

[1] J. W. B. Douglas, *The Home and the School* (London, MacGibbon and Kee, 1964).
[2] H. T. Himmelweit and B. Swift (1969), op. cit.

In deciding to introduce a comparison between schools into our own research we were however handicapped to some extent by our own research design. In the first place, the Himmelweit study was concerned primarily with a comparison between what were essentially grammar and secondary modern schools, with all that that implies in terms of differences in curriculum and objectives, and what we may term the climate of the school. As Himmelweit and Swift themselves express it, 'a grammar and a modern school child live in different worlds as distinct from one another as the world of the manual worker from that of the professional man.' Of the three schools in our study, on the other hand, two were grammar schools. Moreover, although the third school was a comprehensive, for the purpose of comparability we had confined our attention to the academic block, which although containing a proportion of 11-plus 'failures' was following a similar curriculum and preparing to some extent for the same examination. In no sense therefore were we able to replicate the Himmelweit study which was concerned essentially with the differential effect of schools giving substantially different types of education.

A further problem is the use throughout the greater part of our analysis of a criterion of achievement based upon performance in internal examinations. Although the use of such a criterion can be justified for comparisons within schools, it is not possible to use it to throw light upon the influence of the school itself. This requires an external assessment common to all three schools by means of which the achievement of boys in different schools can be compared. The 11-plus results provided us with an external criterion at the start of our investigation and enabled us to compare the entry to the three schools in terms of measured ability and attainment, but no similar means of assessment was available to us once the boys had started at secondary schools until the externally assessed GCE/CSE examination results became available some five years later.

Fortunately the schools took the examinations of the same board and hence the comparison between schools is justifiable. But problems did arise in making the comparison. There is not, for example, comparability between CSE and GCE at all grades although a pass in CSE at grade 1 is deemed to be the equivalent of a GCE pass by the awarding boards. Consequently, for our purposes, all CSE passes *below* grade 1 have been ignored and in quantifying the achievement of the boys in the external examinations only the number of GCE subjects passed has been considered. Differences in the grade of pass were not taken into account. Thus it is possible that some boys had better passes than others, and this should be borne in mind, particularly when comparing the traditional grammar school with the other schools.

Another problem arises in relation to the subjects taken by the boys. Although many of the subjects and syllabuses were common in the three schools, the availability of subjects offered to the boys did differ to some extent. For example, the traditional grammar school offered Greek, Latin, French, German, Spanish and Russian, whereas the other two schools offered only French or German. There was also a much wider choice of technical subjects at both the technical grammar and the comprehensive school. The traditional grammar school offered only woodwork whereas at the other two schools it was possible to take both geometric and engineering drawing and engineering theory and workshop practice as well. This is reflected in Table 7.1 which gives the likelihood of subject passes per boy for each school.

Boys at both the grammar technical school and the comprehensive school were considerably more likely to have passed in a technical subject than boys at the traditional grammar. In comparing number of passes, therefore, we have to take into account the fact that passes at the traditional grammar are more likely to have been in an academic subject. Passes in a foreign language were also not only particularly high at the traditional grammar school, but particularly low at the other two schools. An especially interesting feature of this table is the important part played by technical subjects and science, and to a lesser degree mathematics at the comprehensive school. At the technical grammar, on the other hand, although technical subjects are important English takes the place of science as the subject with the highest number of passes per boy.

Questions can, of course, be raised about the degree to which

Table 7.1 *Percentage number of GCE passes by subject*

Subject	School		
	Traditional grammar	Grammar technical	Comprehensive
English	80	55	20
History/geography/ economics	51	22	12
Languages	84	6	03
Mathematics	50	13	23
Science	58	16	49
Technical subjects	8	47	45
Art and music	10	7	87
Scripture	7	7	7

passes in these various subjects can be considered comparable. Fortunately, some recent research done by the Joint Matriculation Board[1] (whose examinations the boys sat), using a common reference test to monitor the standards of pass in a number of subjects, is reassuring on this score, at least in respect of one year's results. Only four subjects fell outside the tolerance limits of half a grade which they set, and these did not include any of the technical subjects, or the sciences or mathematics. As the authors point out, however, such comparability of standards cannot take into account such factors as the length of course followed, the quality and nature of the teaching given to pupils, the intrinsic difficulty of the subjects or the motivation and interest of the pupils.

A problem of another kind was raised by the very considerable heterogeneity between the three schools in our sample. As we have seen, there were large differences in the ability level of the pupils as measured by IQ and 11-plus scores, with the traditional grammar school boys gaining the highest scores and the boys at the comprehensive school the lowest. Indeed, those boys

[1] G. M. Forrest and G. A. Swift, *Standards in subjects at the O level of the G.C.E.* (JMB, June 1972).

with the lowest scores at the traditional grammar school had similar scores to the very ablest boys at the comprehensive school. Any comparison of GCE/CSE results must therefore hold ability constant if the intention is to measure the effect of the school.

As we have seen, the schools also differed in the social class background of the parents and, as the interviews of the random sample of parents showed, in several other important parental characteristics such as level of aspirations and educational background. Again, therefore, it could not be assumed that differences in examination results between schools were the result of factors in the school itself.

Therefore, after examining the performance of all the boys in the academic classes in the three schools, a group of boys was selected from each school for special study. Within this sample, ability was controlled to a considerable extent by including only those boys whose ability fell within a certain range.[1] In order to control for social class background the sample was divided into middle-class and working-class boys, according to their fathers' occupations. It should be emphasized, however, that because of the difference in the ability level between schools, the boys in the controlled ability sample held very different positions within the school. In the traditional grammar school, for example, they were at or near the bottom of their particular intake in terms of ability, whereas in the comprehensive school they were among the most able boys in their year.

For the purpose of more detailed study a small random sample was drawn from the controlled ability sample. The parents of these boys were interviewed twice, once in the first year and once in the second year. A further interview was planned to take place during the fourth year but it was not possible to complete this plan owing to staffing problems on the research team. From this small sample it has been possible to compare the home background and child-rearing techniques to see to what extent they may be a factor in the different achievement of pupils of the same ability range in different schools.

[1] For a description of the procedure employed see appendix 7, pp. 249-50.

2 THE GCE RESULTS

The first step in the analysis was to compare the GCE results of
all those boys who actually *sat* the examination in each of the
three schools. The average number of passes is shown in Table
7.2. Such a comparison does not however allow for differences in
the proportion of drop-outs, i.e. those boys who did not sit the
examination. There were twelve of these boys at the traditional
grammar school, eight at the technical grammar school, and
nineteen at the comprehensive. The great majority of these were
unsuccessful boys according to our criterion. Although it was
not possible to follow up each of these boys individually, some at
least – as we know from our case studies of unsuccessful boys –
had left at the end of their fourth year at school. When the drop-
outs are included in the analysis, as they clearly should be if we
are to get a complete picture, the mean number of passes per
boy is altered slightly (see Table 7.2), with the comprehensive
school, which had the highest proportion of drop-outs, most
affected.

Table 7.2 *Mean number of GCE/CSE grade 1 passes*

Group	School		
	Traditional grammar	*Grammar technical*	*Comprehensive*
Boys who sat the examination	3·68 (n = 154)	1·97 (n = 78)	2·20 (n = 56)
Total sample including drop-outs	3·41 (n = 142)	1·79 (n = 70)	1·64 (n = 37)
Sample of working-class boys in which ability is controlled	2·33 (n = 52)	1·68 (n = 65)	3·36 (n = 22)

Clearly, therefore, on this analysis the traditional grammar
school is the most successful and the comprehensive school the
least successful. But this is only to be expected when we bear in

mind the differences in the ability level and the social class background of the intake to the three schools. When we look, however, at the controlled ability sample and examine the results of working-class boys only, we get quite a dramatic change in the relative position of the three schools. These are also shown in Table 7.2 and the magnitude of the differences, when tested by one-way analysis of variance, is sufficient to be significant at the 1 per cent level (F = 5·15). Working-class boys at the comprehensive school were more successful than working-class boys of a similar ability range at the other two schools. This is particularly striking since in fact boys from this range of ability who went to the traditional grammar school had a higher mean 11-plus quotient (712·81) than working-class boys who went to the technical grammar school (685·06), and the comprehensive school (670·05). It is possible however that the boys at the traditional grammar school had passes in more academic subjects.

A further analysis was made of middle-class boys within the same range of ability in the traditional grammar school, the only school with a sufficient number of middle-class boys to make this analysis possible. The mean number of passes for each boy, including drop-outs, was 2·47 (n = 17). This is very close indeed to the mean number of passes gained by the working-class boys in the school who were within the same ability range. This suggests that social class factors may be of less importance for this group of pupils than other factors within the school.

One such factor which is common to both working-class and middle-class boys is that of position within the school. It will be recalled that all the boys in the controlled ability sample in this school had a level of ability which was below average for the school as a whole. This is reflected in the school class in which they found themselves as shown in Table 7.3. More than half

Table 7.3 *School class of controlled ability sample*

School	Upper classes	Lower classes
Traditional grammar	16 (3 classes)	36 (3 classes)
Grammar technical	48 (2 classes)	17 (1 class)
Comprehensive	20 (3 classes)	2 (3 classes)

the boys from the traditional grammar school were placed in the three lowest classes, and 83 per cent of these were in the two lowest classes. The school which shows the most obvious proportional difference according to school position in the controlled ability sample is, however, the comprehensive school which had the highest mean pass rate.

Further evidence of the relationship between GCE success and position in the school is provided by an analysis of the performance of the 11-plus successes and 11-plus failures at the comprehensive school. It will be remembered that there were six academic forms or streams at this school, and at the beginning of the first year at the school all the 11-plus successes or 'selected' boys were placed in these streams, together with a number of 11-plus failures selected on the basis of internal tests by the headmaster. Table 7.4 gives the school class of all the intake in the third year, with school class L representing the highest and Q the lowest class in academic terms.

Table 7.4 *The third year school class of 11-plus successes and failures at the comprehensive school*

School class	11+ successes	11+ failures	Total
L and M	22	5	27
N and O	16	11	27
P and Q	6	16	22
Total	44	32	74

It will be seen that, in spite of the absence of any distinction within the school between the two groups (and in fact the teachers did not know the 11-plus results), the 11-plus successes were on the whole much more likely to be in the two top streams, and the 11-plus failures to fall into the two lowest streams. Table 7.5 gives the mean number of GCE passes for each boy by stream, and also as between 11-plus successes and failures.

Table 7.5 *Mean number of GCE passes by stream for 11+ successes and failures*

School class	11+ successes	11+ failures	Total
L and M	3·36	3·80	3·44
N and O	1·19	0·73	0·96
P and Q	0·33	0·13	0·18

There is very little difference *within* streams between 11-plus successes and 11-plus failures, although the difference between streams is very great. It is largely the allocation to streams, therefore, which determines the degree of success in the GCE examinations. Boys in the top two streams have a good chance of success in several subjects, a better chance indeed, as we have seen, than boys of similar ability who were in the lower streams of the traditional grammar school.

It is perhaps worthwhile at this point to comment upon the success rate for the boys at the technical grammar school. The mean number of passes per boy for all the boys, including drop-outs, was 1·79, which was slightly higher than the equivalent figure for the comprehensive school. If we now look at the controlled ability sample of working-class boys we see that the mean number of passes per boy has dropped to 1·68. This is slightly lower than for the group as a whole since boys of very high ability are now excluded. The change is however much smaller for this school than for the other two schools, since the range of ability for our controlled ability sample was the average ability of boys in this particular school. The low success rate of the grammar technical school, in spite of the relatively larger number of boys who were not in the bottom stream, makes the success of the comprehensive school all the more remarkable.

However, before we go on to look more closely at factors within the school for an explanation, it is necessary to consider the possibility that differences in family background, as distinct from the rather crude index of social class based on manual and non-manual occupations, have been responsible for the variation found between schools. In order to do this we must turn to the case studies of the controlled ability sample which will allow us to look for an explanation, not only in terms of socio-economic background, but also in family relationships and techniques of control.

3 THE CASE STUDIES

The random sample of boys selected for intensive study from the controlled ability sample consisted of twelve boys from the traditional grammar school, nine from the technical grammar school, and nine from the comprehensive school. The mean number of GCE passes of those who sat the examination was 1·88 at the traditional grammar school (n = 8), 1·33 at the grammar technical school (n = 6) and 3·35 at the comprehensive school (n = 8). When the 'drop-outs' are included, the advantage of the comprehensive school is relatively increased. These numbers are of course very small, but they reflect quite closely the relative positions of the schools for the controlled ability group as a whole.

Table 7.6 gives the socio-economic status of the boys in each school as measured by father's occupation.

Table 7.6 *Father's occupation of controlled ability case studies in each school*

| Father's occupation | School | | |
	Traditional grammar	Grammar technical	Comprehensive
Non-manual	6	5	1
Foreman	2	1	0
Skilled	3	2	3
Semi-skilled and unskilled	1	1	5

It will be seen that there are differences between the schools of a fairly marked kind which reflect in fact differences in the actual intake to the schools in the year with which we are concerned. Although the numbers are very small, the differences –

particularly between the traditional grammar and the comprehensive schools – are quite striking, especially when we take into account differences within the manual category of occupations. Thus working-class fathers at the traditional grammar school were more likely to be foremen than working-class fathers at the comprehensive school and less likely to be in the semi-skilled or unskilled category. Nevertheless the direction of the differences makes it more difficult to explain the success of the boys at the comprehensive school in terms of socio-economic status. Mother's occupation before marriage showed no differences between schools.

When we turn to social origin as measured by grandfather's occupation the pattern of differences is more complex, as Table 7.7 shows clearly.

Table 7.7 *Social origin of the controlled ability case studies in each school*

Social origin	School		
	Traditional grammar	Grammar technical	Comprehensive
Stable middle	3	0	0
Sunken middle	1	0	5
Socially mobile	3	5	1
Stable working	5	4	3

Stable middle-class parents were found only at the traditional grammar school, again a reflection of the intake to the three schools. Socially mobile parents were found most frequently at the grammar technical school and least frequently at the comprehensive school. What is perhaps most interesting is the high proportion of sunken-middle-class parents at the comprehensive school, and we cannot therefore overlook the possibility that this is a factor in the comprehensive school's success. On the other hand, further information about family background suggests that 'sunken-middle-class' status was not reflected in other aspects of family life. The mean number of siblings for example was 1·4 at the traditional grammar school, o·9 at the grammar technical school and 2·00 at the comprehensive school. Moreover there was very little difference between the schools in the educational background of either mothers or fathers.

Turning now from background factors to parental aspirations we found that these were generally high for all parents, but slightly higher at the traditional grammar school where ten out of twelve mothers and seven out of twelve fathers wanted a university education for their son, compared with four out of nine mothers and four out of nine fathers at each of the other two schools. The relatively low aspirations of parents at the comprehensive school is interesting not only in view of their better GCE performance, but also in the light of the degree of satisfaction with school progress expressed by parents, as shown in Table 7.8.

Table 7.8 *Satisfaction with school progress of controlled ability sample case studies in each school*

Degree of satisfaction	School		
	Traditional grammar	Grammar technical	Comprehensive
High	1	1	3
Fairly high	3	5	5
Low	6	2	1
Very low	2	1	0

Although most parents are fairly satisfied, there is most satisfaction at the comprehensive school and least at the traditional grammar school. This undoubtedly reflects the importance of the school form, since, as we have seen, at the comprehensive school the controlled ability samples were in the highest forms in the school, whereas at the traditional grammar school they tended to be in the lowest forms. The higher aspirations at the traditional grammar school are therefore maintained in spite of a fairly high level of dissatisfaction with school progress. Nor are they simply an aspect of social class background since, for this group of boys, the working-class parents were just as likely to opt for a university as middle-class boys. The aspiration level may however be related to parents' expectations of this particular school which, as we have seen, had very high prestige in the locality and unlike the other two schools had a distinguished record of university scholarships.

Pressure to achieve, as measured by stress on the importance of school progress, by encouragement to try hard and by attention to homework, was assessed at a fairly high level for the majority of boys and there was little difference between schools. Actual help with homework was however considerably more likely at the traditional grammar school where only one boy out of twelve had no help, compared with six out of nine at the comprehensive school. The grammar technical school was intermediate with two out of nine boys getting no help.

Relationships within the family and techniques of discipline showed no pattern of differences between schools. There was also an absence of either the very highly approving parents or the very rejecting and hostile parents found in the case studies of extremely successful and unsuccessful boys. An assessment of the extent to which the boy had internalized parental standards, that is to say the extent to which he appeared to conform to parental wishes over a wide range of aspects of behaviour, also showed little difference between schools although, as Table 7.9 shows, the highest proportion of boys with a low rating was to be found at the traditional grammar school. This may have influenced the boys' progress at school.

Table 7.9 *Internalization of parental standards in each school*

Degree of internalization	School		
	Traditional grammar	Grammar technical	Comprehensive
High or fairly high	5	5	6
Low or very low	7	3	3
No information	0	1	0

All in all, therefore, there is little in the analysis of these case studies to explain the different pattern of success between the schools. With the exception of social origin, all the differences in socio-economic background would lead us to predict that the comprehensive school would be the least successful of the schools. So would the measure of the amount of help with homework which showed that boys at the comprehensive school were getting considerably less help than boys at the traditional grammar school. Indeed from most of these items we would expect the comprehensive school to be less successful than either of the grammar schools. The exception is our rating of the extent to which the boy had internalized parental standards, since the greater non-conformity of boys at the traditional grammar school may well have influenced their progress at school. On the other hand this may itself have been partly a consequence of their position in the school, a point to which we shall return at a later stage in the analysis. It seems reasonable to conclude therefore that the pattern of differences in GCE results must be explained in terms of differences between schools rather than differences in home background.

4 THE SCHOOLS COMPARED

It was not possible, with the resources at our disposal, to make as thorough a study as we would have liked of the schools themselves. Nevertheless, during the four years that we were collecting data for this project, each of the schools was visited many times by members of the research team. The three headmasters were each interviewed formally once, towards the end of the project, but informal discussions took place on many occasions. The boys' form masters were also interviewed during the third year. These interviews, both formal and informal, enabled us to build up a clear picture of the actual organization of the school, and to gain some understanding of the 'climate' of the school.

As we have already indicated, each of the schools was 'streamed' in one way or another, but the manner of streaming, and particularly its timing, was different. The traditional grammar school during the first year had a higher and lower ability band with three parallel classes in each. On the basis of the boys' performance during that year they were separated into three express streams taking a four-year O level course, and three non-express streams taking the normal five-year course. The different express streams were based on subject specialization, not on ability or performance. Of the non-express streams, one contained the 'best' boys but the other two were not differentiated in terms of ability. The boys in the lower streams followed a more limited curriculum, in that they did general science and only one foreign language. It also appears, from the form masters' interviews, that the two lowest forms were explicitly undervalued by some teachers and, in the words of one master, were 'told straight to their faces they are thick'. The headmaster described them as 'not examination material'.

The technical grammar school during the first two years was unstreamed and only at the beginning of their third year were boys divided on the basis of their previous performance into two ability bands. The upper had two parallel classes and the lower was regarded as the bottom stream. This delay in starting streaming did not however appear to alter the situation once the streams had been formed. The lowest of the three classes seems to have been regarded by the staff as of limited ability and difficult to manage. Their form teacher during their third year reported, 'this class is usually the worst in the school; they are usually a bad lot.'

The comprehensive school was, at the time the study was carried out, the most highly streamed of the three schools. Within the academic block there were from the start six streams arranged in order of achievement, and there was also setting for the main subjects. For the first three years there was considerable movement between streams but from the fourth year, when the boys began to prepare seriously for external examinations, the situation became relatively stable. As in the other two schools teacher perceptions and teacher expectations varied between streams. The form master of the lowest of the academic streams in the third year claimed that these boys had all drifted down from higher forms and would probably drift further down, i.e.

into the middle 'block'. This, in his view, was due not to lack of ability but to lack of application. Homework was a problem with this group of boys since, according to this form master, 'you just don't get it. You have to threaten, cane, and then they may bring it in, but if you relax a bit then they go back.' Boys in the top form, L, however, were described as working hard in order to stay where they were. There were no boys persistently involved in homework difficulties, although sometimes a boy would be slow in a particular subject. The form mistress reported, 'I usually get it eventually because most of them are not lazy.' Boys in form M were also described as working well. The form mistress said 'they are anxious; they come and ask me their marks, and do I think they have done any better.'

The three schools therefore had a great deal in common. In each, the bottom stream or streams, although of a very different ability level as measured by both IQ and 11-plus scores, were perceived by the teachers as presenting similar behavioural and academic problems which were seen sometimes as the result of laziness and lack of motivation, at other times of lack of ability. As we have seen in the case of our controlled ability sample, boys of very similar ability performed better in the GCE examination if they were in the top form of the comprehensive school than if they were in the lower form of the traditional grammar school.

In spite of these similarities, the three schools had very different traditions and represented different ideological positions which might be expected to manifest themselves as real differences between the schools. In particular we have already considered in earlier chapters the very good academic record of the traditional grammar school in comparison with the other two schools.

In order to throw more light on these differences a questionnaire was constructed to measure pupils' perceptions of teacher and pupil behaviour.[1] This questionnaire, given to the boys during their third year at the school, was derived from the work

[1] For a fuller report of this part of the study see D. S. Finlayson, 'How high and low achievers see teachers' and pupils' role behaviour', *Research in Education*, III (1970), pp. 38–52.

of Halpin and Croft,[1] although freely adapted to meet our particular needs and circumstances. The items in the questionnaire made up ten scales, five relating to pupil behaviour and five to teacher behaviour. Each item was expressed as a statement about such behaviour. The boys were asked to indicate for each item whether they strongly agreed, agreed, were uncertain, disagreed or strongly disagreed with that statement as an accurate description of the behaviour of pupils or teachers in their school.

A brief description of the scales is given below:

Teacher behaviour scales
Thrust (twelve items) refers to behaviour of teachers which contributes to more effective learning by pupils. This includes their own knowledge of their work, their ability to explain what they mean and their interest in and willingness to help individual pupils who may run into difficulties in their work.

Motivational awareness (twelve items) refers to behaviour which indicates a real concern on the part of teachers to secure the interest of pupils. This includes interest in their own work, their use of motivational devices such as discussion and visual aids, and their ability to relate what is done in class to the interests of the pupils. Although this scale is listed as a teachers' scale, a few items relating to pupils' behaviour are included as indication of the success or otherwise of the teachers' attempt to motivate them.

Consideration (sixteen items) refers to behaviour of teachers which demonstrates their awareness of the individual problems of pupils, and their willingness to adapt their behaviour in the light of pupils' differences.

Use of authority (ten items) refers to behaviour which demonstrates that teachers exercise their authority in such a way that they stifle initiative and spontaneity, make little provision for feedback from pupils, and relate to their pupils in terms of the power they have over them.

[1] A. W. Halpin and D. B. Croft, *Organizational Climate of Schools* (Chicago, Midwest Administrative Centre, University of Chicago, 1963).

Social support (twelve items) refers to behaviour which indicates that teachers actively cultivate warm, friendly relationships with pupils both inside and outside the school and are receptive to any approaches which pupils might make to them about their own personal problems.

Pupil behaviour scales

Esprit (twelve items) refers to behaviour which indicates that some social needs of the pupils are being met as a result of satisfaction derived from work involvement at the school. The items include references to school spirit, satisfaction derived from school work, and antisocial behaviour.

Intimacy (nine items) refers to behaviour indicative of friendly pleasurable relationships among the pupils at games, in school societies, during breaks and outside school.

Engagement (ten items) refers to behaviour which indicates the degree to which pupils constructively participate in the general work of the school as distinct from merely conforming passively to teacher expectations.

Academic orientation (nine items) refers to behaviour which shows concern for academic achievement and includes a willingness to do homework, a keen interest in marks and an acceptance of work as opposed to the pursuit of pleasure.

Hindrance (ten items) refers to the degree to which the provision of books, equipment and staff hinders the pupils from learning. This scale is thus less concerned with social interaction than any of the other scales, and is more related to the material environment in which the interaction takes place.

On a number of the scales there were no differences in the pupils' perceptions of their schools.[1] Pupils in all three schools reported their teachers as equally able to interest them (motivational awareness) and to contribute to their effective learning (thrust). On the other hand in both the technical grammar and comprehensive schools teachers were perceived to have less consideration for pupils' individual needs and to use more autocratic methods of control than at the traditional grammar school. On

[1] See appendix 4, Tables A7.1–3, pp. 239–43.

the pupil scales, boys at the traditional grammar school were perceived as more 'engaged', i.e. more willing to participate in the general work of the school, and more academically orientated. The greater academic orientation of these grammar school boys is not unexpected, in view of the reputation of the school. The fact that they find their masters less strict and more considerate than teachers at the grammar technical and comprehensive schools may reflect differences in teacher behaviour, for presumably it is easier to show consideration to pupils whose behaviour is perceived to reflect their sympathy with the achievement of school goals than to less school-oriented pupils. These differences in pupil and teacher scales may thus be linked.[1]

On the other hand there is little in these differences in the overall comparisons of pupil perceptions between schools to throw fresh light on our findings with respect to GCE results. The greater perceived academic orientation of boys at the traditional grammar school is consonant with the higher success rate in the results of the school as a whole, but not with the poor performance of the controlled ability sample in comparison with the comprehensive school. Similarly, while it is in line with differences between the traditional grammar and the grammar technical school it provides no insight into the technical school's performance *vis-à-vis* the comprehensive school, since the difference in academic orientation between these two schools was small.

A further comparison was made, however, which does link up with the data already presented in this chapter. Using the same analysis of variance design, the perceptions of the groups of successful, achieving as expected and unsuccessful boys in each of the schools |was examined.[2] As in the case of the comparisons between schools, none of the scales produced any significant

---

[1] These scales have now been developed further and extended to include teachers' perceptions. See D. S. Finlayson, 'Measuring school climate', *Trends in Education*, XXX (1973), pp. 19-27. In this article a discussion of the problems associated with the interpretation of data which they produce is presented.

[2] See appendix 4, Table A7.4, p. 243.

overall differences in the perception of successful and unsuccessful boys, although in every school the unsuccessful group of pupils was the least likely to see pupil behaviour in their school as academically orientated. The majority, on the other hand, showed a different pattern of relationships for the perceptions of the successful and unsuccessful groups in each of the schools. Taking the consideration scale as an example, the results are shown in Figure 7.1. In the scale, which shows the tendency in

Figure 7.1 *Mean scores of the differentially successful groups on the consideration scale*

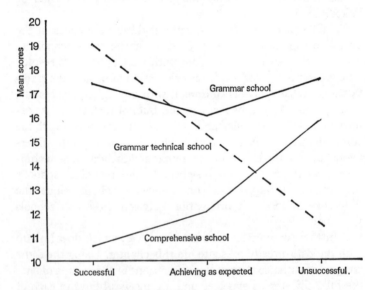

the most marked degree, we find that in the grammar technical school the more successful the group, the more the teachers are seen to be considerate, whereas in the comprehensive school the more successful the group the less consideration the teachers were perceived to show. In the traditional grammar school, however, there were no differences between groups. Other scales, with the exception of academic orientation, showed a similar tendency, with the traditional grammar school groups showing few systematic differences, while the differences in the other two schools were in contrary directions. Thus it was *unsuccessful* pupils at the comprehensive school who had the lowest scores for autocratic control, and the highest scores for warm friendly relationships between teachers and pupils. Similarly it was the *unsuccessful* pupils at this school who rated their teachers highest in terms of 'thrust' and 'motivational awareness'. In the grammar technical school the differences between successful and unsuccessful pupils are even more marked but in this case it is the *successful* pupils who have the consistently more favourable perception of the school.

While at first sight it might appear difficult to reconcile the unfavourable perceptions of the successful comprehensive school pupils with their GCE performance, the explanation seems to lie in the particular school situation in which they found themselves. As we have shown, the comprehensive school, at least at the time this study was made, had an intake of 11-plus successes who were largely borderline. Consequently the 'best' pupils at this school were equivalent in ability to the 'worst' at the traditional grammar school. The effect of this has been well described by one of the form teachers responsible for one of the two top forms. She reports:

We (the teachers) think they (the pupils in her form) are clever, but they are only equivalent to the lower stream in a decent grammar school. Where you have an exam to get through, you have to push the top people, because you have a deadline. If you don't get through the work, and work with the slowest, you are going to penalize the top people, and not get them through.

At this time, too, the school was under considerable constraint to demonstrate the success of the comprehensive experiment, particularly in academic terms. The resultant pressure on the top forms led, as we have seen, to a highly creditable performance at GCE but probably at the cost of a very great deal of hard work and the rigid enforcement of rules.

Unsuccessful boys at the grammar technical school were

found largely in the bottom forms, which as we have seen had the reputation of being difficult to control; the boys' form master seems to have believed that for this reason they needed a particularly firm hand. In particular, he had asked other members of staff to report any trouble they had had with these boys, although this was not the usual practice in the school. He perceived this as an extra means of control over the boys in maintaining that 'the master can deal with them by all means, but then if it comes to me, I have told them I will deal with them as well'. Interestingly, in this connection, the unsuccessful boys at this school had a lower score for 'engagement', i.e. involvement with school, than any other group in any of the schools, and the same was true for academic orientation.

5 CONCLUSION

Before bringing together the main findings of this chapter it is necessary to draw attention yet again to some of the limitations of this study. In the first place the number of pupils involved is small, particularly in the controlled ability sample on which much of the argument rests. In addition only three schools were included in the study, and in any comparison of different types of school we have to hand only one example of each type. Consequently we cannot assume without further evidence that a similar pattern of findings would emerge from a study making use of other schools. It would be highly dangerous, too, to generalize from this particular comprehensive school to comprehensive schools in general, more especially if they had a different kind of intake or had adopted a different form of organization. All that we can hope to do is to throw up hypotheses and suggestions for further research in this area.

This having been said, it remains true that for these particular schools there is evidence that the school itself had an effect on achievement, independent both of ability and home background. This is demonstrated by the GCE success of the comprehensive school boys in the controlled ability sample. Their success cannot be explained in terms of ability since this was controlled, nor in terms of home background since, as we have seen, this tended to be to the advantage of boys from the traditional grammar school.

In seeking for an explanation of these findings it seems likely that the most important factor was the boys' position in the school. This was interpreted differently in each of the three schools according to whether the boy was in the top or bottom stream and according to the school's position in the 'status by pupil ability' hierarchy. All these interpretations appear to be mediated by the general competitive achievement-oriented normative expectations of both teachers and parents.

Associated with these differential interpretations by the teachers of what pupil position in the school actually meant to them there appeared to be fairly definite treatments accorded to the pupils. In all three schools there appeared to be a tendency for teachers to concentrate their attention on the top forms to the academic disadvantage of those at the bottom of the school. The controlled ability sample at the comprehensive school clearly benefited from this pressure although not, as we have seen, without certain disadvantages in terms of pupil/teacher relationships. This differential treatment of pupils in the top forms of the comprehensive school seems to have more than compensated for the absence of a strong academic tradition in the school. Although we have not been able to spell out the actual process in detail this conclusion would seem to provide strong support for the plea of Himmelweit and her associates for more studies of the school in relation to achievement.

CHAPTER EIGHT

AN INTERDISCIPLINARY APPROACH TO SCHOOL ACHIEVEMENT

I THE FRAMEWORK OF ANALYSIS

The main aim of this study was to throw light on the actual process of school achievement. This has been seen as a highly complex and dynamic pattern of relationships involving the home background, the personality and motivation of the child, and the context of the school itself. Although there have been many correlational studies of school achievement, including the longitudinal research carried out by Douglas and his associates, which have made use of variables from these areas, attempts to spell out in detail the interrelationships between the three areas of analysis have been and continue to be rare.

One of the main barriers to the achievement of a conceptual framework of this kind has been, in our view, the failure to develop an interdisciplinary approach to the problem. Appeals for such an approach are not of course new, and indeed are made very frequently, particularly by those working in the more applied aspects of the social sciences. It must also be admitted that attempts at interdisciplinary research have seldom been successful, since they rarely mean more than the application of several disciplines to the same problem but with the researchers working quite independently or by one discipline assuming a dominant position to determine the concepts and methodology selected.[1] In the work carried out by Douglas and his team, for example, psychological, sociological and even biological variables were all included, but little attempt was made to develop concepts or adopt a methodology which would allow the study of the interaction between them.

In attempting to develop a genuine interdisciplinary framework the present research has used concepts derived from both psychology and sociology not as alternative hypotheses in whch 'personality' and 'social structure' are seen as rival explanatory factors, but as interrelated aspects of a single process. Similarly, this is in no sense an exercise in reductionism, whether psychological or sociological. In attempting to understand how some of the boys have been successes and others failures we have sought continually to examine ways in which social structure and personality are in interaction.

The pattern which emerges from the hierarchical analysis demonstrates a particular set of relationships between sociological and psychological variables very clearly. A number of measures of personality such as introversion, intellectual curiosity and dependence on adults are found to be linked to parental warmth and approval, parental perception of and satisfaction with success at school, parental aspiration and parental perception of the boy's ability. It has been suggested, moreover, that it is not possible to conceive of either the parental measures or the pupil attributes as 'causes' as there seems to be a complex process of interaction involved in which parental approval could be interpreted as both cause and consequence of the performance of the boy at school and his behaviour at home. The delineation of the details of this interaction process are beyond the resources of this project, but the case studies of the successful working-class boys have made its complexity clear.

There are, however, limitations in this study which may have a significant bearing on our analysis. Some of these have been discussed in detail in earlier chapters and need only be referred to briefly here. The use of extreme groups, the definition of

[1] D. S. Finlayson, 'Value judgements and research criteria', in G. Chanan (ed.), *Research forum on teachers' education* (NFER, 1972), pp. 48–55.

school achievement adopted, the ability range of the pupils, their sex and age must all be recognized as limitations on the generality of the findings, as is the small number of schools involved. Yet a further point to be considered is the omission of some variables altogether from the analysis. Some, like Bernstein's linguistic codes, were excluded from the beginning as requiring more resources than we had at our disposal. Others had to be abandoned at an early stage because the collection of the necessary data involved more problems than we were able to cope with. One area which had to be abandoned in this way was what, following Jackson and Marsden, we had called 'knowledge of the system'. Several measures were devised which it was hoped would tap this area, but none was satisfactory. In drawing up the profiles of successful and unsuccessful boys there may well be a number of additional factors which are related to school achievement. Similarly, in the hierarchical analysis we have included in the main only those variables which have been found to be related to achievement for our particular sample. Other variables such as neuroticism have been shown to interact with them. In the discussion of our findings and their implications which follows, these limitations should therefore be kept in mind.

2 SOCIAL CLASS AND SCHOOL ACHIEVEMENT

The relationship between social class and socio-economic status and school achievement has been well established, and in this respect our findings were not unexpected. What is perhaps more surprising is the strength of the relationship found, when we bear in mind that the system of allocation to secondary schools had produced considerable homogeneity *within* schools. In some respects, for example, the working-class parents with sons at traditional grammar schools were more like middle-class parents of pupils at that school than like working-class parents with sons at the other schools.

The main emphasis in this study of course has been on the reason for this relationship between social class and achievement, but – as the detailed analysis of our findings has shown –

an examination of several aspects of socio-economic status believed to be causal agencies has shown them *not* to be related to school achievement for our particular sample. This was so, for example, with family size, probably because this item did not discriminate within schools. It implies nevertheless that family size cannot be used to explain the differences in achievement found in our study. Mother's occupation was also found not to be related to achievement, although this item did in fact discriminate well. It is not clear why this should have been so for this sample, when other studies have frequently pointed out the significance of this variable, but it may have something to do with the actual type of occupation followed by these mothers. Many of them in fact were doing clerical work of a fairly routine and unskilled kind. Income, too, although closely related to father's occupation and discriminating well within schools, showed only a fairly slight tendency to be related to achievement. Paternal grandfather's occupation, and parental educational background did, however, show quite a marked relationship with achievement.

On the other hand, as we have seen, the hierarchical analysis indicated a relationship between social class background, patterns of child-rearing and achievement motivation or drive, which carries the possible implication that middle-class boys were more successful at school because they had a greater drive for achievement; a drive which may well have been developed or encouraged by the use of love-oriented techniques of discipline on the part of the parents. This is in line with earlier studies, particularly those carried out by Rosen and d'Andrade described previously. The case studies of the successful working-class boys also point to the significance of child-rearing techniques in differentiating between successful and unsuccessful boys *within* the working-class group. Moreover, although parental educational experience was related to success for the sample as a whole, this appears to be only because middle-class parents were both more successful and more highly educated than working-class parents. Within the working classes, differences in educational experience were not related at all to school achievement. Indeed, within our admittedly small sample of extreme groups, the most educated of the working-class parents had *unsuccessful* sons. On the other hand it may be that the amount of further or higher educational experience within the working class was not sufficient to make any difference since it was only the exceptional working-class parents who had more than a very limited amount of further education.

Nor, as we have argued previously, can we explain social class differences, at least to any considerable extent, in terms of differences in parental aspirations. Although there was a relationship between level of aspirations and success, the comments of the parents themselves during the interviews suggested quite strongly that these were to a large extent dependent on their perception of the boy's progress at school. Moreover the actual level of aspiration of these parents was very high, indeed much higher than the actual results of these boys in the GCE examination subsequently justified. The majority of fathers of boys in the extremely unsuccessful group even as late as the boys' fourth year at school wanted them to have some form of further full-time education. The scaling down of aspirations which had taken place was in fact mostly from university to technical college or college of education.

Even more striking is the picture presented by the case studies of working-class boys and their parents. As we have seen, the majority of parents of the unsuccessful boys were deeply involved in their son's progress, and many were highly ambitious for their future success which they saw as compensating for their own relative failure. Consequently, although the absence of such an involvement may well be prejudicial to high achievement our findings suggest that its presence is no guarantee at all against failure. Indeed the most bitter quarrels in these families centred upon the failure of the boy to respond to the pressure to achieve placed upon him by his parents, and the interviews in some of their homes were deeply unhappy experiences for researcher and respondent alike. Some of the implications of this for educational policy will be discussed in a subsequent section (see pp. 187–92).

Also of interest was the finding that parents of successful working-class boys were no more likely to be sunken-middle-class than parents of unsuccessful boys, nor except in the secondary technical school, more likely to have fathers who were foremen. This, together with the fact that they were no more likely to have had more educational experience, raises the question, which unfortunately cannot be answered here, why these particular parents made use of techniques of discipline which, as this study and many others have indicated, are more typical of middle-class families. It does appear reasonable to assume however that their use of these particular techniques was a factor in the highly successful performance of their sons at school.

At the same time, there are at least hints in the case study material that the warm, loving and highly approving parents of these successful boys were responding, in part at least, to the behaviour of their sons who seemed, from the interviews, to be ready to conform to adult expectations to an unusually high degree. Similarly the severe punishment meted out by the parents of many unsuccessful boys was at times at least a despairing reaction to a long history of conflict and even rebellion over parental authority. This is *not* to suggest that the discipline techniques used by parents can be seen in any simple way as a response to behaviour which has its source elsewhere. There are examples in the case studies of very different responses from parents towards the same behaviour, for example with respect to smoking. Parents also had very clear ideas about what were and what were not permissible techniques of discipline, some being horrified at the very idea of smacking and others using it frequently as a matter of course. There were signs too that the extreme conflict between some fathers and their sons could be attributed to the very open hostility and absence of emotional warmth displayed by these fathers towards their sons. What seems to be the case therefore is that the relationship between patterns of parental discipline and the behaviour of the boy can only be understood in terms of a lengthy process of interaction in which the response of the child tends to reinforce parental behaviour, just as the actions of the parents tend to encourage certain behaviour in the child. In order to understand the process of achievement therefore we need to take into consideration not only the background of the home but also the personality and motivation of the child.

3 THE ROLE OF PERSONALITY AND MOTIVATION

We have already described the kind of boy likely to be successful rather than unsuccessful according to our definition of success and failure. Perhaps one of the more noticeable features of this profile is the important part played in it by the boy's motivation to succeed, whether this is measured as an internal drive or in terms of a questionnaire assessment of expressed achievement values. At the same time the successful boys had higher educational aspirations, although we have suggested that these may in part have been a reflection of their previous success.

The interviews with parents indicated too that the successful boys gave little trouble over homework, which indeed they tended on the whole to take very seriously, spending significantly more time on it than did unsuccessful boys. The measure of homework orientation, indeed, had the highest tau value of the pupil variables. Judging from the parental interviews, the unsuccessful boys with few exceptions tended to do less homework as the school years went by, until in the fourth year many seemed to be doing very little work at home and some none at all. The actual conditions under which homework was carried out ranged from a warm well-appointed room alone to the crowded family living-room with a background of television or radio, but we failed to find any relationship between these conditions and success or failure. What seemed to be important was the internal motivation of the boy himself.

The case studies also demonstrated that the unsuccessful boys tended generally to be more non-conformist than successful boys, and this is borne out to some extent by the questionnaire measure of dependent proneness. Successful boys tended to be more dependent on adults and therefore, we may assume, more anxious to try to secure their approval by conforming to their values and expectations. For these boys, as we have suggested earlier, success at school must be seen as part of a much wider tendency to try to please their parents.

The higher scores of the successful boys on the measures of intellectual curiosity also suggest, however, that their acceptance of homework may not have been entirely due to their conforming tendencies. The long hours spent on their homework may well have had for them an intrinsic satisfaction denied to those boys whose interests were of a less intellectual kind. The fact that the unsuccessful boys were more likely to be extraverts, preferring to be with others rather than to spend time alone and, in the two grammar schools, taking an interest at an earlier age in the company of girls, also helps to explain their lack of staying power with respect to homework.

The origin of this intellectual interest still remains to be explained, however, particularly when we recall how little evidence of such an interest was manifested in most of their homes. It may be that we have to look at other agencies, including the schools, for the influencing factor. The precise part played by the introversion/extraversion dimension of personality, and its relationship not only with intellectual curiosity but also with the various measures of achievement, also requires further examination. In the hierarchical analysis, introversion and intellectual curiosity were linked together, whereas achievement motivation was associated with the social class variables and techniques of discipline. It may be, therefore, that introversion and intellectual curiosity on the one hand, and achievement motivation on the other, are different and even alternative paths to high achievement. Further research with a larger sample would be needed to test the validity of this hypothesis.

Perhaps the most important conclusion of this study therefore is to underline the need for a comprehensive theory of motivation which is applicable to education. The evidence has indicated that the motivation leading to success in the school context is multidimensional, and there are of course likely to be many additional motives which have not been assessed in this study. This suggests that any adequate formulation of a theory of motivation must be highly complex. Nevertheless without it our understanding of the process of achievement is unlikely to proceed very much further than it has at present.

The analysis of the working-class successful and unsuccessful

G

boys also makes clear that certain boys were successful just because they had developed the necessary personality and motivation which appears to be necessary to succeed. As we have suggested earlier, intellectual curiosity, introversion, dependence on adults, conformity and an internalized drive to succeed may all, singly or together, have played a part, and the interrelationship between these factors has still to be explored more fully in relation to achievement. The reason why some working-class boys developed these particular aspects of their personality or character is also not yet fully understood, although it has been suggested here that techniques of discipline adopted by the parents may be an important factor. The case for a more adequate investigation into the relationship between personality and social structure would therefore seem to have been made, and the study of social class differences in achievement cannot, it seems to us, be profitably undertaken within any but an interdisciplinary framework.

4 THE SCHOOL CONTEXT

The study of the part played by the school itself in achievement has necessarily been limited for reasons which have already been outlined. Briefly, we were handicapped by the fact that we had only three schools in our sample; schools which, moreover, in spite of their differences, had in common the academic curriculum of the selective secondary school. Furthermore, time and resources limited the amount and kind of data we could collect and we were unable in particular to make any observations of the interaction between teachers and pupils in the actual classrooms. Comparison between the schools was also made more difficult by the differences in the range of ability and in the socio-economic background of the intake into the three schools. In order to overcome some at least of these problems we made a more detailed analysis of those boys falling within the same band of ability in all three schools, a group which we have called the controlled ability sample. A small number of boys were randomly selected from this group in each of the schools for the purpose of throwing some light on differences in home background.

Since these boys represented different ability levels in each school the effect was to make our comparison more complex, since we were comparing boys holding different positions within different schools.

The comparisons of GCE results for the whole sample of boys in the three schools showed the pattern that might have been expected, bearing in mind the ability range of the pupils and their socio-economic background. The mean number of passes per boy was highest at the traditional grammar school and lowest at the comprehensive school. When we look at the results of the controlled ability sample, however, the pattern is changed dramatically and it is now the comprehensive school which has the highest success rate, and the grammar technical school which has the lowest. But the differences in the patterns of the subjects in which passes were obtained must be borne in mind. The boys in the traditional grammar school studied more languages while the boys at the grammar technical and comprehensive schools entered for more subjects in the science and technical fields.

We have offered evidence that the higher success rate of boys at the comprehensive school was related to the position of these boys within the school. These boys were, as we have seen, in the highest ability range in the year's intake to the school and were found to be in the top forms. In consequence their own expectations and the expectations of both teachers and parents seem, from the evidence we have, to have been raised. They appear, too, to have been thought of by their teachers as well-behaved hardworking boys even if they were not thought of as very clever. The boys in the controlled ability sample at the traditional grammar school had the lowest ability of the boys in their year; consequently they suffered from the comparison with the other boys in the school. In the lowest forms they had the reputation, in the eyes of some of the staff, of being 'thick' and there was little confidence in their ability or expectation of their examination success. The case studies of the parents also suggest that the parents too were disappointed in what they saw as a lack of ability in their sons. It should be noted however that these boys performed better than the boys in the same ability group at the grammar technical school. We have not been able to explain the relatively low performance of boys at this school in terms either of home background or the boy's position in the school, and it may be that the different traditions of the two grammar schools were the operative factor.

Other features of the comprehensive school may also have contributed to these very successful GCE results. The school was new and well equipped, particularly for technical subjects – claims which could also be made for the technical grammar school. Another important feature of the comprehensive school at this time was a very strong desire on the part of the staff to 'prove' the success of comprehensive education, and this may have meant extra pressures on the top boys to demonstrate that academic achievement was not beyond the reach of pupils at their school. This point might be resisted on ideological grounds by maintaining that academic achievement is not the only concern of comprehensive schools. The evidence of the form teachers and the parents, however, demonstrates clearly that they were very much concerned with it.

The comments of the form teachers in all the schools, taken together with the evidence from the scales which quantify the boys' perceptions of their teachers, indicate that teachers have different expectations about pupils' achievement according to the school class they happen to be in, and also that they appear to behave differently towards pupils according to their expectations.

The evidence that we have does not permit any definite conclusions to be drawn about the way in which these expectations were distributed among the staff nor precisely how they related to teachers' behaviour. Other possibilities which might account for the differences in the achievement levels between the schools must always be considered. One of these is that the different pattern of subjects offered by the boys at the comprehensive school has some motivational characteristics not inherent in the more academic and linguistic pattern which was characteristic of the grammar school boys. If this is so, it is difficult to explain the relatively poor performance of the boys in the grammar technical school whose subject pattern was more similar to the comprehensive school than the grammar school.

Though we are unable to be specific about the precise reason for the differential performance of our controlled ability sample according to the school they attended, we have provided evidence that the school can, under certain circumstances, be *more important* than home background in explaining differences in school achievement. The boys in the controlled ability sample at the traditional grammar school did less well than boys at the comprehensive school in spite of the fact that differences in socio-economic status favoured the boys at the traditional grammar school. Clearly, therefore, the belief which has gained currency mainly as a consequence of the evidence of the Plowden Report that the school is of little importance in comparison with home background in its effect on achievement is by no means true in all contexts. It has been suggested by Finlayson elsewhere[1] that one of the reasons for the Plowden conclusions is that the procedures adopted by the researchers engaged in the major surveys for that report were determined more by the methodologies available and approved of by their professional reference groups than by the nature of the problems which the Plowden Committee was set up to investigate. However that may be, our evidence, in line with that of Himmelweit, suggests at the very least that further study into the role of the school in relation to the achievement of pupils is urgently needed. When it is undertaken, it will be important to discuss the criteria which determine the choice of the research strategy.

5 EDUCATIONAL IMPLICATIONS

In some ways it might be argued that any discussion of the educational implications of this study is not justified in view of the exploratory nature of the research and the limitations of the sample. Certainly the generality of our findings to different schools is suspect without further research. Nevertheless, provided this is kept very much in mind, it would appear to be useful to consider the implications of our findings for those pupils who have been 'under-achieving' in terms of their ability. These 'under-achieving' pupils, it will be noted, were to be found not

[1] D. S. Finlayson, (1972), op. cit., p. 51.

only in our extremely unsuccessful groups of boys but also in the controlled ability sample of boys at the traditional grammar and technical grammar schools, since in comparison with the boys in their ability group at the comprehensive school they were clearly 'under-achieving'.

In attempting to deal precisely with this problem the Plowden Report tried to distinguish between background factors (such as parental education) which are not amenable to change, and 'attitudinal' factors which are at least open to change, if the way can be found. Of these attitudinal variables, the most important in the report's view was parental aspirations. It was also assumed in Plowden that the direction of the relationship was from parental aspirations to child's achievement. This study, based it is true on data from secondary and not, as in Plowden, from primary education, has suggested that the relationship also tends to operate in the opposite direction and that parental *and* pupil aspirations are in part at least dependent on school achievement. The adoption of such a view[1] moreover does not seem inconsistent with the evidence in Plowden that the relationship between aspirations and achievement, starting off as very slight with the infant group, increases with age. Presumably it is only after parents have obtained evidence of how their child is faring at school that they begin to set relative aspirations for him or her. Bernstein and Brandis have also reported that working-class mothers seem to give more stimulation and support in their education to those children who are thought to be 'bright'.[2] It may be that the parents and pupils involved in our study are particularly sensitive to this type of feedback, there being an almost total absence of traditional middle-class and markedly socially deprived families in our sample, where presumably the cultural influences on aspirations are at their strongest and aspirations may be presumed to be more stable.

[1] D. S. Finlayson, 'Parental aspirations and the educational achievement of children', *Educational Research*, XIV (1) (1971), pp. 61–4.
[2] B. Bernstein and W. Brandis, 'Social class differences in communication and control' in W. Brandis and D. Henderson (eds.), *Social Class Language and Communication* (London, Routledge and Kegan Paul, 1970), pp. 93–123.

If it is accepted that the major component of what Plowden called 'attitudinal' factors is not prior to but, to some extent at least, consequent upon actual achievement, then the educational consequences of such a view are far-reaching. The degree to which such attitudes are directly open to persuasive change is radically reduced. This view appears to be supported by empirical evidence from Plowden itself[1] as well as by our evidence. In the former, the achievement of pupils in schools having favourable parent/school relationships was no different from those in which such contacts were minimal. This finding certainly raises doubts as to whether the emphasis which Plowden places on the raising of parental 'attitudes' for the improvement of children's achievement is really merited. Our evidence, particularly among the parents of unsuccessful working-class boys at the two grammar schools, showed that high parental aspirations can produce most unfortunate consequences. The aspirations of the working-class parents had been raised by their boys' success in the 11-plus and when these aspirations were not borne out by the boys' actual achievements the parents were bitterly disappointed. In some cases the boys were punished for poor marks or poor reports and, even in the absence of actual punishment, were frequently subjected to a barrage of criticisms about their failure at school. It would seem wrong therefore to place too much reliance on raising parental ambitions without at the same time improving the chances of their children achieving success.

It may be that high parental aspirations to be effective in relation to achievement require to be associated with affection and sensitivity on the part of the parents. These factors are part of what we have called the emotional climate of the home and, together with techniques of child-rearing, are related to achievement. But we have suggested that the actual pattern of relationships involved is a highly complex one, and it is unlikely that the emotional climate of a home can be readily changed from outside. Often too, the boys' low achievement was itself influencing relationships within the family. Some of the personality characteristics of the boys themselves also appear to be of a fairly enduring and stable kind. Although the source of aspects of

[1] D. S. Finlayson (1971), op. cit., p. 63.

personality such as introversion/extraversion and dependence on parents may be problematic, it seems likely that, in so far as they are environmentally determined, this takes place at a very early stage in the development of the personality. The motivational variables similarly appear to have their origins in certain kinds of parent/child interaction and presumably these too would be difficult to influence directly, although little or no work appears to have been done on the degree to which early experiences in school might contribute to the development of a need for achievement in children.

We have treated intellectual curiosity as an intrinsic form of motivation in which intellectual activities are rewarding in themselves. The ability of the school to provide learning experiences which motivate the pupils would appear to be of special consequence for those pupils who are not motivated in any other way, for example by a need for achievement. Presumably, too, the more that school work has this inherent motivation for pupils the less relevant or the less necessary will other types of motivation be. Few studies have included assessments of the degree to which schools are successful in this respect, and some American studies have concluded that this intrinsic motivation or interest in school work for its own sake is not a factor in school achievement.[1] Yet our study suggests that in the context of the kind of academic curriculum which was typical of all three of our schools, intellectual curiosity may be important and one of the ways in which a school can *directly* contribute to the success of its pupils is by creating for them inherently motivating learning experiences. To say this is not to make any constructive suggestion about how such motivation is to be achieved, but empirical justification for such an emphasis is provided.

Most of the comments about the educational implications of the findings relate to pupils as individuals, interacting with parents at home and teachers in school. But in the section which examined the achievement of the controlled ability sample it was shown that the boy's position in the structure of the school is

[1] See for example J. A. Kahl 'Common man boys' in A. H. Halsey, J. Floud and C. A. Anderson (eds.), *Education, Economy and Society* (Glencoe, Ill., Free Press, 1961).

also related to his achievement. From our study, it is not possible to come to any conclusion about the reasons for this influence, but from the evidence of the interviews with the form teachers it is clear that teachers have different expectations for their pupils according to their position in the school and, in the case of the comprehensive school, according to the school's position in relation to other schools within the educational system. According to the form teacher's reports and the evidence derived from the pupils' perceptions of the behaviour of the teachers, these expectations which the teachers have would seem to be associated with the way in which pupils in different classes in the school are actually treated.

Further research is clearly necessary if the process which results in school achievement is to be better understood. What is important about the evidence from this study is not the conclusions we have tentatively drawn but the directions in which our findings suggest that research might go. In particular the evidence from the controlled ability sample clearly implies the significance of the school, and indeed the actual classroom situation as an area for further study. This conclusion indicates that studies in depth of the school itself as a factor in achievement are urgently needed. The details of such research cannot be mapped out here, but organizational factors within schools, such as methods of grouping pupils, and status considerations between schools would have to play their part. This latter aspect is of current interest if grammar and comprehensive schools are to continue to coexist. The relationship of these factors to the expectations that teachers have about pupils, how their expectations affect their overt behaviour and how they communicate their expectations to pupils are additional matters for study.

Equally important however is the need to study the way that schools as well as parents motivate children to learn. We have no studies within the school which parallel the attempt of Rosen and d'Andrade to understand how parents encourage their children to want to succeed. Only by such means as this can we eventually hope to understand the part played by the school as well as the home in the development of what has sometimes been called the achievement syndrome.

Finally, attempts to assess in general terms whether factors in the home background or in the school are more important in school achievement are unlikely to be fruitful in exploring those areas of educational endeavour which are within the control of educators and which are likely to influence the level of school achievement. Statistical criteria which emphasize the importance of large samples drawn from many different kinds of school have given rise to conclusions which, at the level of individual schools, can be seriously misleading. What this study has demonstrated, more than anything else, is the necessity for focusing research attention on the interaction effects between pupils, the homes they live in and the schools which they attend. The ways in which the effects of the home relate to the personality and motivation of the child and how these in turn relate to the effects of the school are essentially part of a two-way dynamic process. If this view was given more recognition then the design of educational research studies would begin to reflect some of the complexities of the achievement process.

APPENDIX 1

The method of selecting the random sample was not identical in each of the three schools. Adaptations in the method were made which seemed appropriate to the peculiarities of the pupil population and to the main aims of the study. Two of the factors which were regarded as of significance in the study were measures of general ability and social class. Accordingly in respect of both these variables, when it was considered necessary, a stratified form of sampling was used. For clarity, the methods used in each of the schools will be described separately.

In the grammar school, after excluding all boys who did not have two parents living at home and a few other special cases, a one-in-three sample was drawn from 140 boys. In order that the sample should adequately reflect the social class and ability standard of the year group, the boys were stratified into three ability levels according to their 11-plus verbal reasoning test scores – 120, 120–9 and 130+. Within each of these ability levels, the children were split into four groups according to father's occupation. Group 1 included professional occupations, group 2 other non-manual occupations, group 3 foremen and skilled workers and group 4 unskilled. Within each of the twelve cells so obtained, a one-in-three sample was drawn. The numbers in the final sample, totalling 47, are shown in Table A1.

Table A1 *Grammar school sample*

Verbal reasoning score	Social class			
	Professional	Other non-manual	Foremen and skilled	Unskilled
130+	3	3	3	2
120–9	9	6	6	3
–120	3	3	3	3

In the grammar technical school, the number of professional and other non-manual families amounted to less than 25 per cent of the school population. As a social class analysis would not be worthwhile, the population was stratified according to verbal reasoning scores. After four boys whose families were disturbed were excluded, a one-in-two sample from the remaining eighty-six was made. The distribution of the total sample of forty-six is given below:

Table A2 *Grammar technical school sample*

Verbal reasoning score	Number
130+	5
120–9	10
110–19	25
–110	6

In the comprehensive school, the policy was to run certain forms as academic streams. Into these went those boys who had passed the 11-plus and who were, hence, considered capable of a grammar school course. To this number were added an almost equal number of boys who were selected by the school on the basis of an internal examination.

Of most concern, therefore, in this school appeared to be an adequate representation of selective and non-selective boys who were undertaking the academic courses. Hence, after excluding six boys from broken families a one-in-two sample was made in each of these groups and the following numbers obtained.

Table A3 *Comprehensive school sample*

Selected	21
Non-selected	18
Total	39

APPENDIX 2

THE SELECTION OF THE GROUPS OF SUCCESSFUL AND UNSUCCESSFUL BOYS

As age allowances are made in the 11-plus tests, the influence of age was examined in the examination scores for the first year. A decision was required at the end of this year about whether to make a similar allowance for the boys' examination scores, and hence no other years were examined. One-way analysis of variance was used in each school across age groupings but in no school was there any evidence that the older boys obtained higher examination results. It was decided therefore to make no age allowance in respect of any of the examination scores.

Correlations between the 11-plus quotients and the school examinations in each of the three schools showed coefficients of roughly the same order of magnitude in each of the schools. All are in the medium range, so that there will inevitably be a considerable margin of error involved in prediction.

In order to make the degree of such error explicit, the standard error of the predictions made from each regression equation was calculated so that the degree of confidence associated with the magnitude of particular differences between the predicted and actual scores could be indicated. This was done on an interval basis, going from greater to lesser degrees of probability. The two extreme difference intervals were readily determined—those falling within the limits of the probable error (50 per cent of confidence) and those in excess of the 5 per cent level of confidence. Three intervening intervals of roughly equal areas of probability were chosen as shown in Table A4, in order to secure a normal distribution of interval scores.

Differences, of course, would be either positive or negative, and hence ten intervals, also shown in Table A4, were available for characterizing the difference scores.

Table A4 *Intervals corresponding to degrees of confidence*

Probability of error	Intervals	
	+	−
5%	1	10
5–19%	2	9
20–33%	3	8
34–50%	4	7
>50%	5	6

By this method, all difference scores falling in categories 5 and 6, being less than the probable error, can be regarded as due largely to chance. The pupils having such difference scores (50 per cent of the school groups) were then held to have achievements in line with prediction. Those boys whose achievement scores exceeded their predicted scores by more than the probable error, intervals 1–4, were regarded as successful. Those boys whose achievement scores were less than their predicted scores by more than the probable error, intervals 7–10, were regarded as unsuccessful.

It is important to realize that only two of these intervals – 1 and 10 – represent a difference between predictive and actual achievement of sufficient magnitude to fall within the usual 5 per cent confidence limits. Hence, if only one difference score were treated in this way, the chances of wrongly regarding a number of children in intervals 7–9 as unsuccessful, in intervals 5 and 6 as achieving as expected, and in intervals 2–4 as successful are still fairly high. To minimize errors of chance of this kind, the rounded mean interval score of each child in each of the three school examinations was taken as the final criterion of success. In a very small number of cases where there was a *consistent* trend over the three years for a pupil's interval score to go up or down, then the final interval score and not the mean was taken as the score most likely to represent that child's final achievement status in school.

School achievement scores

The scores in four internal academic subject examinations – English, maths, science and a foreign language – were used in the examination of personality effects in order to equate achievment areas. In each school one common paper was given to all classes in most of the subjects and scripts were marked by the same marker throughout. The marks in each subject were then standardized within each school separately, using units which caused as little disturbance to the original scores as possible. In the few cases where different papers were given in any subject, the marks were scaled prior to standardization. The total of the four standardized subject marks was then taken as the second measure of school achievement.

APPENDIX 3

Because of the large amount of data derived from individual items, both in the interview schedules and from questionnaires, special mention will be made of the procedure which was adopted for the treatment of the responses. Following the checking of the accuracy of the coding categories the responses were punched on computer tape for subsequent analysis. This was carried out in four stages with both the interview and questionnaire item data.

Stage 1 : item relationship with success/unsuccess
In the first instance each item was run against the successful/unsuccessful categorization. The categories used with the first year extreme groups were those derived from the first year predictions, and with the third year extreme groups, the cumulative categories were used. In order to maximize the number of cases in each scoring category all the responses were dichotomized. This was done separately for each of the schools since, although the total numbers were relatively small, it was considered necessary in order to ascertain whether the same tendencies were manifest in all three schools.

With the first year data, the Fisher Exact Probability Test

was used on each of the 2×2 tables produced. Subsequently a computer programme was written to deal with the third year data, using χ^2 rather than the Fisher Exact Probability Test. Each item was again tested for the significance of its relationship with success/unsuccess. Because of the reduced likelihood of error in the selection of the third year groups, and because of limited resources, further analysis was mainly confined to the third year data.

Those items showing a positive relationship with success and unsuccess were grouped together in clusters. The criteria employed in allocating items to these clusters were:

(i) that in terms of face validity, at least, all the items in a cluster should be related to a common aspect of experience and behaviour

(ii) that any item should be significantly related to success or unsuccess in at least one school, preferably in more

(iii) that if no significant relationship emerged, items should have tendencies towards significance, particularly if a similar trend was observed in at least two schools.

Stage 2: inter-item relationship

The items included in each cluster were now related one with another, using χ^2 to test the significance of the relationship. The testing of the interrelationships among the items was intended to demonstrate whether the initial selection of items on the basis of their face validity was in fact justified. This process of item selection was used in preference to factorial analysis of the interview data for two reasons. The first was that the number of items involved was too great for the available computer to handle. The second was that the score distribution of a number of the items was not sufficiently symmetrical to justify the use of correlational methods.

A further pruning of items took place at this stage. Only those items which were significantly related to 50 per cent or more of the other items in that cluster were retained. In a few cases the 10 per cent level of significance was regarded as acceptable. In the great majority of cases, however, the percentage was very much higher than 50 per cent and the level of significance 5 per cent or above. When the number of cases in any cell was less than five, Yates correction was used.

As a result of this two-phase procedure, in which empirical relationships are used to reinforce face validity, a number of clusters were produced.

Stage 3: cluster scoring

Once the necessary relationship of each item to both success in school and to other items in its particular cluster had been established the categories used to score each item were examined and, as far as possible, adapted so that each item within every cluster had the same range of scoring possibilities. This was done in order to give equal weight to items within clusters. Hence, cluster scores obtained by adding the item scores can be regarded as assessments employing interval units.

Cluster scores were obtained for each boy and his parents by summing his scores in each of the cluster items. In the case of any boy or parent for whom a score for any item was not available, they were given the rounded mean score for that item obtained by all the other interviewees from this particular school. These scores were then subjected to further analysis, depending on the purpose and groups involved.

For the items included in questionnaires given to all the boys, the procedure followed the same three stages as with the extreme group data. The main difference was that the population used to test each item against the success criterion was the total one. The cumulative success interval scores were used and each item was run against the successful (1–4), achieving as expected (5 and 6), and unsuccessful (7–10) categories. Following the establishment of a relationship with success, the same criteria as with the extreme group data were employed in the creation of clusters, and cluster scores were obtained.

THE CLUSTERS

Details of each of the clusters obtained in this way are now given, values of p being indicated as follows:–

$$op = < \cdot 10$$
$$*p = < \cdot 05$$
$$**p = < \cdot 01$$
$$***p = < \cdot 001$$

1 χ^2 *values of items in Parental Examination Expectations cluster*
  1 Examination expectations, father
  2 Examination expectations, mother

$$\chi^2 = 24 \cdot 09**$$

2 χ^2 *values of items in Parental Examination Aspirations cluster*
  1 Examination aspirations, father
  2 Examination aspirations, mother

$$\chi^2 = 18 \cdot 79**$$

3 χ^2 *values of items in Parental Higher Educational Aspirations cluster*
  1 Higher educational aspirations, father
  2 Higher educational aspirations, mother

$$\chi^2 = 32 \cdot 16**$$

4 χ^2 *values of items in Parental Perception of Boy's Ability cluster*
  1 Perception of boy's ability, father
  2 Perception of boy's ability, mother

$$\chi^2 = 20 \cdot 16**$$

5 χ^2 *values of items in Parental Perception of Boy's Progress cluster*
  1 Perception of boy's progress, father
  2 Perception of boy's progress, mother

$$\chi^2 = 31 \cdot 05**$$

6 χ^2 *values of items in Boy's Educational Goal Achievement cluster*

Table A5 *Grammar School*

	1	2	3	4
1	–	36·22**	25·02**	5·48°
2		–	28·36**	13·04**
3			–	21·64**
4				–

Table A6 *Grammar technical school*

	1	2	3	4
1	–	10·68**	11·79**	13·00**
2		–	7·41*	6·13°
3			–	14·13**
4				–

Table A7 *Comprehensive school*

	1	2	3	4
1	–	28·73**	6·27*	7·72*
2		–	11·61**	12·58**
3			–	3·70°
4				–

1 Examination aspirations
2 Examination expectations
3 Higher educational aspirations
4 Vocational aspirations

Table A8 *Coding of Pupil Aspiration and Expectation items*

Item	*Dichotomy*	
Examination aspirations	Beyond A level	Up to and including A level
Examinations expectations	At least A level	Up to and including O level
Further educational aspiration	Full-time	Part-time
Vocational aspiration	Professional	Other

7 χ^2 *values of items in Boy's Homework Orientation cluster*

Table A9

	1	2	3	4
1	–	6·88**	15·52**	9·45**
2		–	5·57*	3·27⁰
3			–	17·81**
4				–

1 Time spent on homework
2 Response to homework by boy
3 More time on homework now
4 More trouble over homework now

8 χ^2 *values of items in Material Level of Home cluster*
  1 Income
  2 Father's further education

$$\chi^2 = 3\cdot27^{\circ}$$

9 χ^2 *values of items in Mother's Education cluster*
  1 Mother's secondary education
  2 Mother's further education

$$\chi^2 = 13 \cdot 51^{**}$$

10 *Parental reading code*	*Code number*
Serious reading by both parent, including serious magazines as well as books	1
Serious reading as above by one parent only	2
Interest in reading books, by at least one parent but not serious reading	3
Interest in magazines and newspapers by one or both parents	4
No interest in books or magazines – popular newspapers only	5

11 χ^2 *values of items in Parental Perception of Boy's Problem cluster*

Table A10

	1	2	3	4	5
1	–	17·68**	12·16**	9·09**	2·92°
2		–	28·00**	23·00**	8·03**
3			–	42·42**	4·08*
4				–	4·56*
5					–

  1 Problems in primary school
  2 Problems in first year
  3 Problems in second year
  4 Problems in third year
  5 Problems in fourth year

12   χ^2 *values of items in Nature of Relationships cluster*

Table A11

	1	2	3
1	–	19·73**	45·21**
2		–	20·83**
3			–

1 Father's demonstration of affection
2 Mother's sensitivity to needs of child
3 Father's sensitivity to needs of child

13   χ^2 *values of items in Parental Approval cluster*
    1 Pride and approval, mother
    2 Pride and approval, father

$$\chi^2 = 62\cdot25**$$

14   χ^2 *values of items in Parental Satisfaction with School Progress cluster*
    1 Satisfaction with school progress, father
    2 Satisfaction with school progress, mother

$$\chi^2 = 25\cdot03**$$

15   χ^2 *values of items in Parental Use of Shouting, Threatening, etc. as a Method of Control cluster*
    1 Mother's use of shout, threats
    2 Father's use of shout, threats

$$\chi^2 = 13\cdot67**$$

16   χ^2 *values of items in Parental Use of Smacking as a Method of Control cluster*
    1 Mother's use of smacking
    2 Father's use of smacking

$$\chi^2 = 9\cdot43**$$

17 χ^2 *values of items in Parental Use of Material Deprivation as a Method of Control cluster*
1 Mother's use of material deprivation
2 Father's use of material deprivation

$$\chi^2 = 35 \cdot 47^{**}$$

18 χ^2 *values of items in Mother's Use of Non-psychological Methods of Control cluster*

Table A12

	1	2	3
1	–	5·97*	2·24
2		–	3·15°
3			–

1 Mother's use of shout, threats, etc.
2 Mother's frequency of smacking
3 Mother's material deprivation

χ^2 *values of items in Father's Use of Non-psychological Methods of Control cluster*

Table A13

	1	2	3
1	–	3·53⁰	6·72*
2		–	3·51°
3			–

1 Father's use of shout, threats etc.
2 Father's frequency of smacking
3 Father's use of material deprivation

19 χ^2 *values of items in Lack of Interest in Girls cluster*

Table A14 *Grammar school*

	1	2	3
1	–	30·50**	29·62**
2		–	46·03**
3			–

Table A15 *Grammar technical school*

	1	2	3
1	–	20·62**	19·92**
2		–	25·65**
3			–

Table A16 *Comprehensive school*

	1	2	3
1	–	12·03**	2·53
2		–	9·63**
3			–

1 Girls among best friends
2 Would like to spend time with girls
3 Actually spends time with girls

APPENDIX 4

Note Values of p are indicated as follows:–

$$^\circ = p = < \cdot 10$$
$$* = p = < \cdot 05$$
$$** = p = < \cdot 01$$
$$*** = p = < \cdot 001$$

CHAPTER 2

1 *Extraversion and neuroticism*

Table A2.1 *Mean scores of personality groups on extraversion, neuroticism and verbal reasoning*

School	Degree of Neuroticism	Test	Extra-verts	Intro-verts
Grammar		No. in group	32	32
	Low	Ext/Int	21·34	16·13
	neuroticism	Neur.	7·00	7·50
		VRQ	126·00	126·44
		No. in group	32	32
	High	Ext/Int	21·44	16·00
	neuroticism	Neur.	14·91	16·31
		VRQ	125·22	124·50

School	Degree of Neuroticism	Test	Extra-verts	Intro-verts
Grammar Technical	Low neuroticism	No. in group	14	14
		Ext/Int	21·93	16·00
		Neur.	8·79	8·71
		VRQ	116·71	118·00
	High neuroticism	No. in group	14	14
		Ext/Int	21·43	14·50
		Neur.	16·50	17·29
		VRQ	118·00	119·71
Comprehensive	Low neuroticism	No. in group	15	15
		Ext/Int	21·40	12·80
		Neur.	7·20	5·53
		VRQ	108·20	108·33
	High neuroticism	No. in group	15	15
		Ext/Int	21·40	16·20
		Neur.	14·87	16·33
		VRQ	107·67	109·13

Table A2.2 *Mean score of all personality groups in 11-plus tests*

School	Degree of Neuroticism	EQ means		AQ means	
		Extra.	Intro.	Extra.	Intro.
Grammar	Low	118·81	121·84	124·09	124·94
	High	121·28	120·00	123·16	122·50
Grammar technical	Low	111·36	113·57	117·29	112·29
	High	112·14	113·64	119·07	119·43
Comprehensive	Low	106·47	104·40	109·40	107·00
	High	106·13	108·47	108·20	109·67

Table A2.3 *Grammar school personality group examination means*

Degree of Neuroticism	1st year		2nd year		3rd year	
	Extra.	Intro.	Extra.	Intro.	Extra.	Intro.
Low	187·50	223·59	194·37	232·62	190·50	235·87
High	191·22	195·82	180·72	206·09	171·78	210·84

Table A2.4 *F ratios of personality effects in grammar school*

Effect	1st year	2nd year	3rd year
Extraversion	3·21	9·70**	14·6**
Neuroticism	1·12	3·87	3·9*
Interaction	1·92	< 1	< 1

Table A2.5 *Grammar technical school personality group examination means*

Degree of Neuroticism	1st year		2nd year		3rd year	
	Extra.	Intro.	Extra.	Intro.	Extra.	Intro.
Low	375·86	420·79	372·21	435·79	371·64	428·71
High	391·79	436·21	390·86	439·14	397·50	422·93

Table A2.6 *F ratios of personality effects in grammar technical school*

Effect	1st year	2nd year	3rd year
Extraversion	4·80*	6·12*	4·09*
Neuroticism	< 1	< 1	< 1
Interaction	< 1	< 1	< 1

* Significant at 5 per cent level.

Table A2.7 *Comprehensive school personality group examination means*

Degree of Neuroticism	1st year		2nd year		3rd year	
	Extra.	Intro.	Extra.	Intro.	Extra.	Intro.
Low	190·00	200·67	194·73	193·13	199·80	196·53
High	207·53	214·40	207·20	204·33	209·93	216·20

Table A2.8 *F ratios of personality effects in comprehensive school*

Effect	1st year	2nd year	3rd year
Extraversion	< 1	< 1	< 1
Neuroticism	2·46	1·6	2·10
Interaction	< 1	< 1	< 1

Table A2.9 *Means and F ratios from third year extreme groups on extraversion*

School	Successful group means	Unsuccessful group means
Grammar	15·56	19·22
Grammar technical	17·25	20·00
Comprehensive	16·89	19·22

F ratios

Between groups	8·88**
Between schools	< 1
Interaction	< 1

Table A2.10 *Means and F ratios from third year extreme groups on neuroticism*

School	Successful group means	Unsuccessful group means
Grammar	14·11	13·44
Grammar technical	11·88	11·50
Comprehensive	13·00	10·78

F ratios

Between groups	< 1
Between schools	< 1
Interaction	< 1

2 *Dependent proneness*

Table A2.11 *Means and F ratios from third year extreme groups*

School	3rd year extreme groups	
	Successful group means	*Unsuccessful group means*
Grammar	19·11	17·44
Grammar technical	22·25	18·88
Comprehensive	18·22	17·89

F ratios	
Between groups	2·28
Between schools	1·87
Interaction	1·15

Table A2.12 *Means and F ratios from third year extreme group scores from adult and peer-group items of dependent-proneness test*

School	Adult items		Peer-group items	
	Successful group means	*Unsuccessful group means*	*Successful group means*	*Unsuccessful group means*
Grammar	9·78	7·33	5·89	4·78
Grammar technical	9·63	7·00	5·38	5·75
Comprehensive	7·11	7·11	5·56	5·11

F ratios

Between groups	4·29*	< 1
Between schools	1·29	1·16
Interaction	2·28	< 1

3 Reaction to rules about friends and hair

Table A2.13 *Boys' reaction to parental rules about friends: first year and third year extreme groups*

School		1st year extreme groups		3rd year extreme groups	
		Co-operative	Uncooperative	Co-operative	Uncooperative
Traditional	S	11	2	10	1
grammar	US	3	8	6	3
Grammar	S	6	4	6	2
technical	US	2	8	4	7
Compre-	S	5	5	7	3
hensive	US	0	7	6	3
Combined	S	22	11	23	6
	US	5	23	16	13

Table A2.14 *Boys' reaction to parental rules about hair: first year and third year extreme groups*

School		1st year extreme groups		3rd year extreme groups	
		Co-operative	Uncooperative	Co-operative	Uncooperative
Traditional	S	8	5	7	2
grammar	US	3	7	2	4
Grammar	S	7	3	5	0
technical	US	4	6	4	3
Compre-	S	5	5	6	0
hensive	US	0	7	5	2
Combined	S	20	13	18	2
	US	7	20	11	9

4 *Homework orientation*

Table A2.15 *Amount of time spent on homework*

School		1st year extreme groups		3rd year extreme groups	
		¾ hour or above a night	Below ¾ hour a night	¾ hour or above a night	Below ¾ hour a night
Traditional	S	11	1	11	0
grammar	US	9	2	6	3
Grammar	S	9	1	8	0
technical	US	4	6	5	6
Comprehensive	S	9	1	10	0
	US	3	4	2	7
Combined	S	29	3	29	0
	US	16	12	13	16

Table A2.16 *Boys' acceptance of homework : first and third year extreme groups*

School		1st year extreme groups		3rd year extreme groups	
		Accepting	Rejecting	Accepting	Rejecting
Grammar	S	7	6	8	3
traditional	US	4	7	4	5
Grammar	S	5	5	7	1
technical	US	3	5	4	7
Comprehensive	S	8	1	5	5
	US	4	1	2	7
Combined	S	20	12	20	9
	US	11	13	10	19

Table A2.17 *Change in amount of time spent on homework : third year extreme groups*

School		3rd year extreme groups	
		More time	Less or the same time
Traditional	S	9	1
grammar	US	1	5
Grammar	S	5	1
technical	US	1	6
Comprehensive	S	6	3
	US	2	6
Combined	S	20	5
	US	4	17

Table A2.18 *Change in amount of trouble taken over homework : third year extreme groups*

School		3rd year extreme groups	
		More trouble	Less or the same trouble
Traditional	S	7	3
grammar	US	2	4
Grammar	S	5	0
technical	US	0	6
Comprehensive	S	6	3
	US	2	6
Combined	S	18	6
	US	4	16

Table A2.19 *Means and F ratios from third year extreme group scores on homework orientation*

School	3rd year extreme groups	
	Successful group means	*Unsuccessful group means*
Grammar	4·67	5·89
Grammar technical	4·88	6·75
Comprehensive	5·44	7·00

F ratios	
Between groups	23·02***
Between schools	3·02
Interaction	< 1

5 *Intellectual curiosity*

Table A2.20 *Means and F ratios from third year extreme group scores on intellectual curiosity*

School	3rd year extreme groups	
	Successful group means	*Unsuccessful group means*
Grammar	11·11	5·22
Grammar technical	9·63	5·00
Comprehensive	8·11	4·56

F ratios	
Between groups	29·69***
Between schools	1·57
Interaction	1·27

Table A2.21 *Mean scores and F ratios of success groups in all
schools in intellectual curiosity scale*

Group	School		
	Grammar (n = 153)	Grammar technical (n = 80)	Comprehensive (n = 69)
Successful	8·42	8·52	8·00
Achieving as expected	7·49	8·38	8·18
Unsuccessful	6·46	6·91	6·41
F ratio	2·47	1·78	1·75

6 Interests

Table A2.22 *Mean scores and F ratios: Lack of Interest in
Girls cluster*

School	Successful	Unsuccessful
Traditional grammar	5·89	4·33
Grammar technical	5·38	4·63
Comprehensive	5·56	5·33

F ratios

Between groups	13·03***
Between schools	1·30
Interaction	5·67**

7 *Achievement orientation*

Table A2.23 *School means and F ratio for BICR questionnaire*

Grammar (n = 156)	Grammar technical (n = 87)	Comprehensive (n = 73)	F ratio
14·21	13·87	13·01	3·05*

Table A2.24 *Means and F ratios for third year extreme groups on BICR questionnaire*

School	3rd year extreme groups	
	Successful group means	Unsuccessful group means
Grammar	12·33	14·44
Grammar technical	15·13	13·25
Comprehensive	13·67	13·56

F ratios

Between groups	< 1
Between schools	< 1
Interaction	5·31**

Table A2.25 *School means and F ratio for future/present questionnaire*

Grammar (n = 156)	Grammar technical (n = 88)	Comprehensive (n = 78)	F ratio
7·55	6·69	6·35	8·69**

Table A2.26 *Mean scores and F ratios for third year extreme group scores on future/present orientation*

School	3rd year extreme groups	
	Successful group means	*Unsuccessful group means*
Grammar	8·11	6·67
Grammar technical	7·13	7·50
Comprehensive	7·22	5·78

F ratios

Between groups	2·38
Between schools	1·01
Interaction	2·14

CHAPTER 3

1 *Expressed achievement motivation*

Table A3.1 *Mean and F ratios for third year extreme groups*

School	3rd year extreme groups	
	Successful group means	*Unsuccessful group means*
Grammar	11·67	7·44
Grammar technical	12·63	6·63
Comprehensive	10·44	9·67

F ratios

Between groups	15·18***
Between schools	< 1
Interaction	5·53**

Table A3.2 *Mean expressed achievement motivation scores of the successful and unsuccessful groups*

Groups		Successful		Unsuccessful	
Neuroticism		High	Low	High	Low
N/achievement	High	11·18	10·88	7·53	9·35
	Low	10·41	7·71	8·41	11·12

Table A3.3 *Analysis of variance table for expressed achievement motivation scores*

Source	df	Sum sq.	Mean sum sq.	F ratio
Neuroticism	1	4·97	4·97	< 1
N/achievement (N/ach)	1	3·55	3·55	< 1
Success	1	30·11	30·11	2·73
N × N/ach	1	4·98	4·98	< 1
N × S	1	120·47	120·47	10·92**
N/ach × S	1	92·25	92·25	8·36**
N × N/ach × S	1	23·05	23·05	2·09
Within groups	128	1411·88	11·03	
Total	135	1691·26		

** $P = < ·01$

2 Aspirations and expectations

Table A3.4 *Mean and F ratios for third year extreme group scores in Educational Goal Achievement cluster*

School	3rd year extreme groups	
	Successful group mean scores	Unsuccessful group mean scores
Grammar	3·11	3·78
Grammar technical	3·50	4·38
Comprehensive	3·67	4·89

F ratios	
Between groups	10·79**
Between schools	3·08
Interaction	< 1

Table A3.5 *Means and F ratios for third year extreme group scores in Parental Educational Aspiration cluster*

School	3rd year extreme groups	
	Successful group mean scores	Unsuccessful group mean scores
Grammar	2·00	2·56
Grammar technical	2·37	2·87
Comprehensive	2·22	3·11

F ratios	
Between groups	10·06**
Between schools	1·47
Interaction	< 1

Table A3.6 *Means and F ratios for third year extreme group scores in Parental Higher Educational Aspiration cluster*

School	3rd year extreme groups	
	Successful group mean scores	Unsuccessful group mean scores
Grammar	2·11	3·11
Grammar technical	2·75	3·75
Comprehensive	2·67	3·22

F ratios	
Between groups	9·76**
Between schools	1·3
Interaction	< 1

Table A3.7 *Means and F ratios for third year extreme group scores in Parental Educational Expectations cluster*

School	3rd year extreme groups	
	Successful group mean scores	Unsuccessful group mean scores
Grammar	2·11	2·56
Grammar technical	2·37	3·00
Comprehensive	2·44	3·55

F ratios	
Between groups	12·56***
Between schools	3·62*
Interaction	1·93

3 Aspirations, expectations and achievement

Table A3.8 *Means and F ratios from third year extreme group scores in Parental Perception of Boy's Ability cluster*

School	3rd year extreme groups	
	Successful group mean scores	Unsuccessful group mean scores
Grammar	2·11	3·00
Grammar technical	2·63	3·50
Comprehensive	2·78	3·22

F ratios	
Between groups	16·69***
Between schools	2·06
Interaction	<1

Table A3.9 *Means and F ratios for third year extreme group scores in Parental Perception of Boy's Progress cluster*

School	3rd year extreme groups	
	Successful group mean scores	Unsuccessful group mean scores
Grammar	2·00	3·22
Grammar technical	2·50	3·50
Comprehensive	2·11	2·89

F ratios	
Between groups	23·61***
Between schools	2·09
Interaction	< 1

4 *Longitudinal study*

Table A3.10 *Changes in examination aspirations according to third year stream membership*

Aspirations in 2nd year	3rd year stream	3rd year aspirations	
		A level	O level
A level		1	10
O level	Lower	1	10
A level		26	12
O level	Upper	4	5

Table A3.11 *Changes in examination expectations according to third year stream membership*

Expectations in 2nd year	3rd year stream	3rd year expectations	
		A level	O level
A level		1	10
O level	Lower	1	10
A level		18	12
O level	Upper	8	9

Table A3.12 *Changes in higher educational aspirations according to third year stream membership*

Aspirations in 2nd year	3rd year stream	3rd year aspirations	
		Full-time	Part-time
Full-time		8	10
Part-time	Lower	1	3
Full-time		23	9
Part-time	Upper	9	6

Table A3.13 *Changes in vocational aspirations according to third year stream membership*

Aspirations in 2nd year	3rd year stream	3rd year aspirations	
		Professional	Other
Professional		2	6
Other	Lower	1	7
Professional		15	3
Other	Upper	13	8

CHAPTER 4

1 *Love/hostility dimension*

Table A4.1 *Means and F ratios, Nature of Relationship cluster*

School	3rd year extreme groups	
	Successful	Unsuccessful
Traditional grammar	4·44	6·22
Grammar technical	5·63	6·38
Comprehensive	6·56	6·67
F ratios		
Between groups	2·93	
Between schools	2·12	
Interaction	1·83	

Table A4.2 *Mean scores and F ratios, Parental Approval cluster*

School	3rd year extreme groups	
	Successful	Unsuccessful
Traditional grammar	2·89	3·78
Grammar technical	2·88	4·50
Comprehensive	3·78	4·22
F ratios		
Between groups	8·08**	
Between schools	1·35	
Interaction	2·01	

Table A4.3 *Means Scores and F ratios, Parental Satisfaction with School Progress cluster*

	3rd year extreme groups	
School	Successful	Unsuccessful
Traditional grammar	2·00	3·22
Grammar technical	2·38	3·38
Comprehensive	2·11	3·11
F ratios		
Between groups	27·65***	
Between schools	<1	
Interaction	<1	

2 *Control/autonomy dimension*

Table A4.4 *Mean parental autocratic/democratic scores of third year extreme success/unsuccess groups*

Group	Mothers			Fathers		
	Successful mean	Unsuccessful mean	't'	Successful mean	Unsuccessful mean	't'
Grammar	38·00 (n = 11)	54·00 (n = 6)	2·72*	45·27 (n = 11)	55·50 (n = 6)	2·51*
Grammar technical	50·57 (n = 7)	57·00 (n = 9)	2·07	55·83 (n = 6)	59·44 (n = 9)	<1
Comprehensive	46·44 (n = 9)	46·20 (n = 5)	<1	54·63 (n = 8)	54·14 (n = 7)	<1

Table A4.5 *Correlation of parental autocratic/democratic attitudes with boys' success scores*

School	N	Mother	Father
Grammar	38	·379*	—·087
Grammar technical	31	·297	·147
Comprehensive	32	—·125	—·044

Table A4.6 *F ratios of mean scores of mothers' use of non-psychological methods of control*

School	3rd year extreme groups	
	Successful	Unsuccessful
Traditional grammar	4·00	4·67
Grammar technical	3·75	4·75
Comprehensive	4·56	5·33
F ratios		
Between groups	9·95**	
Between schools	2·95	
Interaction	<1	

Table A4.7 *Mean scores and F ratios of fathers' use of non-psychological methods of control.*

School	3rd year extreme groups	
	Successful	Unsuccessful
Traditional grammar	3·78	4·89
Grammar technical	4·00	4·63
Comprehensive	4·78	4·78
F ratios		
Between groups	4·20*	
Between schools	1·18	
Interaction	2·71	

CHAPTER 5

1 *Socio-economic status*

Table A5.1 *Mother's occupation: first year and third year extreme groups*

School	Success group	1st year groups		3rd year groups	
		non-m	m	non-m	m
Traditional	S	12	1	7	4
grammar	US	6	4	5	4
Grammar	S	3	7	2	6
technical	US	5	5	6	5
Comprehensive	S	4	5	5	5
	US	3	4	4	5
Combined	S	19	13	14	15
	US	14	13	15	14

Table A5.2 *Paternal grandfathers' occupation: first year and third year extreme groups*

School		1st year groups		3rd year groups	
		nm	m	nm	m
Traditional	S	11	2	6	5
grammar	US	2	8	0	9
Grammar	S	3	7	2	6
technical	US	0	9	1	9
Comprehensive	S	4	6	4	6
	US	2	5	1	8
Combined	S	18	15	12	17
	US	4	22	2	26

Table A5.3 *Maternal grandfathers' occupation: first year and third year extreme groups*

School		1st year groups		3rd year groups	
		nm	m	nm	m
Traditional	S	4	7	5	6
grammar	US	3	7	3	6
Grammar	S	1	8	2	6
technical	US	0	9	0	11
Comprehensive	S	1	8	1	8
	US	0	9	3	6
Combined	S	6	23	8	20
	US	3	25	6	23

Table A5.4 *Parental income: first year and third year extreme groups*

School		1st year extreme groups		3rd year extreme groups	
		Below £1,000 p.a.	Above £1,000 p.a.	Below £1,000 p.a.	Above £1,000 p.a.
Traditional	S	4	9	3	7
grammar	US	6	5	4	5
Grammar	S	6	5	4	4
technical	US	7	4	6	3
Compre-	S	6	4	4	2
hensive	US	7	1	7	2
Combined	S	16	18	11	13
	US	20	10	17	10

Table A5.5 *Family size: first year and third year extreme groups*

School		No. of children: 1st year groups		No. of children: 3rd year groups	
		1–2	3+	1–2	3+
Traditional	S	10	3	5	6
grammar	US	6	5	3	6
Grammar	S	5	5	5	3
technical	US	3	7	4	7
Comprehensive	S	3	7	2	8
	US	2	5	3	6
Combined	S	18	15	12	17
	US	11	17	10	19

Table A5.6 *Random sample: family size by fathers' occupation*

Size of family	Traditional grammar Fathers' occ.		Grammar technical Fathers' occ.		Compre-hensive Fathers' occ.		Combined Fathers' occ.	
	nm	m	nm	m	nm	m	nm	m
I child	6	3	4	3	–	3	10	9
2 children	9	9	5	10	–	3	14	22
3 children	5	9	5	7	1	14	11	30
4 or more	2	3	0	9	3	14	5	26

Table A5.7 *Random sample: family size of selective and non-selective comprehensive school boys*

No. of children	Selective boys	Non-selective boys
1–3	16	5
4 or more	5	12

2 *Educational level of home*

Table A5.8 *Random sample; fathers' secondary education by fathers' occupation*

School attended	Traditional grammar		Grammar technical		Comprehensive		Combined	
	Fathers' occ.		Fathers' occ.		Fathers' occ.		Fathers' occ.	
	nm	m	nm	m	nm	m	nm	m
Selective	11	2	4	2	0	6	15	10
Non-selective	10	21	10	27	4	28	24	76

Table A5.9 *Random sample: mothers' secondary education by fathers' occupation*

School attended	Traditional grammar		Grammar technical		Comprehensive		Combined	
	Fathers' occ.		Fathers' occ.		Fathers' occ.		Fathers' occ.	
	nm	m	nm	m	nm	m	nm	m
Selective	4	7	2	2	1	5	7	14
Non-selective	16	15	12	27	3	29	31	71

Table A5.10 *Random sample: fathers' further education by fathers' occupation*

Type of education	Traditional grammar		Grammar technical		Comprehensive		Combined	
	Fathers' occ.		Fathers' occ.		Fathers' occ.		Fathers' occ.	
	nm	m	nm	m	nm	m	nm	m
Full-time	8	8	8	9	2	15	18	32
Part-time	10	6	5	6	1	5	16	17
None	4	10	1	13	1	13	6	36

Table A5.11 *Random sample: fathers' qualifications by fathers' occupation*

Qualifications	Traditional grammar		Grammar technical		Comprehensive		Combined	
	Fathers' occ.		Fathers' occ.		Fathers' occ.		Fathers' occ.	
	nm	m	nm	m	nm	m	nm	m
Yes	16	7	8	6	1	9	25	22
No	6	17	6	23	3	24	15	64

Table A5.12 *Random sample: further education by fathers' occupation*

Type of further education	Traditional grammar		Grammar technical		Comprehensive		Combined	
	Fathers' occ.		Fathers' occ.		Fathers' occ.		Fathers' occ.	
	nm	m	nm	m	nm	m	nm	m
Full-time	9	5	2	5	0	6	11	16
Part-time	3	5	1	5	1	3	5	13
None	10	14	11	19	3	25	24	58

Table A5.13 *Random sample: mothers' educational qualifications by fathers' occupation*

Qualifications	Traditional grammar		Grammar technical		Comprehensive		Combined	
	Fathers' occ.		Fathers' occ.		Fathers' occ.		Fathers' occ.	
	nm	m	nm	m	nm	m	nm	m
Yes	7	4	4	5	0	5	11	14
No	15	20	10	24	4	29	29	73

Table A5.14 *Fathers' secondary education: first year and third year extreme groups*

School		1st year extreme groups				3rd year extreme groups			
		Non-selective		Selective		Non-selective		Selective	
		F	M	F	M	F	M	F	M
Traditional grammar	S	5	9	8	4	3	6	8	4
	US	10	11	1	0	8	8	1	1
Grammar technical	S	8	8	2	2	7	6	1	2
	US	9	10	1	0	9	10	2	1
Compre-hensive	S	8	6	2	4	8	8	2	2
	US	7	7	0	0	7	9	2	0
Combined	S	21	23	12	10	18	20	11	8
	US	26	28	2	0	24	27	5	2

Table A5.15 *Parents' experience of further education: first year and third year extreme groups*

School		1st year extreme groups				3rd year extreme groups			
		None		Some		None		Some	
		F	M	F	M	F	M	F	M
Traditional grammar	S	4	5	9	8	4	6	7	5
	US	6	11	5	0	6	9	3	0
Grammar technical	S	7	7	3	3	6	7	2	1
	US	8	8	2	2	7	8	4	3
Compre-hensive	S	5	8	5	2	4	8	6	2
	US	7	6	0	1	6	7	3	2
Combined	S	16	20	17	13	14	21	15	8
	US	21	25	7	3	19	24	10	5

Table A5.16 *Random sample: parental reading by fathers' occupation*

Reading habits	Fathers						Mothers					
	Grammar		Technical		Comprehensive		Grammar		Technical		Comprehensive	
	Fathers' occ.		Fathers' occ.		Fathers' occ.		Fathers' occ.		Fathers' occ.		Fathers' occ.	
	nm	m	nm	m	nm	m	nm	m	nm	m	nm	m
Regular readers	12	13	5	11	1	10	8	8	6	6	2	11
Occasional or non-readers	10	11	9	18	3	24	14	16	8	23	2	23

Table A5.17 *Random sample: parental library membership by fathers' occupation*

Library membership	Fathers						Mothers					
	Grammar		Technical		Comprehensive		Grammar		Technical		Comprehensive	
	Fathers' occ.		Fathers' occ.		Fathers' occ.		Fathers' occ.		Fathers' occ.		Fathers' occ.	
	nm	m	nm	m	nm	m	nm	m	nm	m	nm	m
Yes	7	10	9	5	1	7	11	8	6	5	2	11
No	15	14	5	24	3	27	11	16	8	24	2	23

Table A5.18 *Random sample: type of magazines by fathers' occupation*

Magazines	Traditional grammar		Grammar technical		Comprehensive		Combined	
	Fathers' occ.		Fathers' occ.		Fathers' occ.		Fathers' occ.	
	nm	m	nm	m	nm	m	nm	m
Technical or educational	17	14	8	13	2	10	27	37
Other	5	10	6	16	2	24	13	50

Table A5.19 *Parents' reading code: first year and third year extreme groups*

School		1st year extreme groups			3rd year extreme groups		
		Non-readers	Non-serious readers	Serious readers	Non-readers	Non-serious readers	Serious readers
Traditional grammar	S	2	6	5	1	4	6
	US	4	7	0	4	5	0
Technical grammar	S	2	7	1	3	3	2
	US	9	1	0	9	1	1
Compre-hensive	S	5	4	4	5	4	1
	US	5	6	0	0	5	0
Combined	S	9	17	10	9	11	9
	US	18	14	0	13	11	1

Table A5.20 *Amount of Parental Help with Homework: first year extreme groups*

Subject	Success category	Fathers		Mothers	
		Some help	No help	Some help	No help
Maths	Successful	28	5	18	15
	Unsuccessful	13	15	9	19
Languages	Successful	16	17	16	17
	Unsuccessful	8	20	9	19

Table A5.21 *Amount of Parental Help with Homework : third year extreme groups*

Subject	Success category	Fathers		Mothers	
		Some help	No help	Some help	No help
Maths	Successful	9	20	7	22
	Unsuccessful	7	22	4	25
Languages	Successful	5	24	11	18
	Unsuccessful	2	27	2	27

Table A5.22 *Mothers' Education cluster*

School	3rd year extreme groups	
	Successful group means	Unsuccessful group means
Grammar	3·11	3·89
Grammar technical	3·63	3·75
Comprehensive	3·56	3·78
F ratios		
Between groups	4·67*	
Between schools	<1	
Interaction	2·63	

Table A5.23 *Material Level of Home cluster*

School	3rd year extreme groups	
	Successful group means	*Unsuccessful group means*
Grammar	2·67	3·11
Grammar technical	3·25	3·25
Comprehensive	3·11	3·44
F ratios		
Between groups	1·73	
Between schools	1·54	
Interaction	< 1	

CHAPTER 7

Table A7.1 *Means and F ratios derived from scales related to the needs of individual pupils*

Group	Scale	School		
		Grammar	Grammar technical	Compre-hensive
Successful	Esprit	23·53	24·53	19·80
	Intimacy	22·50	20·00	19·73
	Thrust	26·90	28·73	21·33
	Consideration	17·43	18·80	10·73
Achieving as expected	Esprit	22·03	22·17	22·27
	Intimacy	21·60	18·80	22·23
	Thrust	24·52	24·73	22·90
	Consideration	16·00	15·00	12·07
Unsuccessful	Esprit	21·50	17·05	22·15
	Intimacy	22·70	15·60	22·45
	Thrust	26·70	20·55	25·65
	Consideration	17·48	11·25	15·65
Total	Esprit	22·22	21·14	21·66
	Intimacy	22·15	18·09	21·72
	Thrust	25·74	21·37	23·39
	Consideration	16·79	14·72	12·86
F ratios	Schools	Esprit	< 1	
		Intimacy	13·44**	
		Thrust	1·96	
		Consideration	7·92**	
	Success groups	Esprit	1·99	
		Intimacy	< 1	
		Thrust	< 1	
		Consideration	< 1	
	Interaction	Esprit	9·33**	
		Intimacy	10·76**	
		Thrust	12·08**	
		Consideration	16·62**	

Table A7.2 *Means and F ratios derived from scales related to social control*

Group	Scale	School		
		Grammar	Grammar technical	Compre- hensive
Successful	Engagement	21·13	21·07	17·87
	Social warmth	27·63	26·27	19·53
	Use of authority	19·13	19·47	26·47
Achieving	Engagement	20·40	19·03	17·27
as	Social warmth	25·60	25·23	24·90
expected	Use of authority	21·12	22·63	24·87
Unsuccess-	Engagement	20·43	14·00	18·85
ful	Social warmth	28·10	20·30	26·00
	Use of authority	20·05	24·95	21·85
Total	Engagement	20·59	17·95	17·89
	Social warmth	26·84	23·95	24·00
	Use of authority	20·12	22·62	24·31
F ratios	Schools	Engagement	6·61**	
		Social warmth	3·31*	
		Use of authority	8·74**	
	Success groups	Engagement	1·74	
		Social warmth	<1	
		Use of authority	<1	
	Interaction	Engagement	11·96**	
		Social warmth	12·05**	
		Use of authority	11·04**	

Table A7.3 *Means and F ratios derived from scales relating to motivation*

Group	Scale	School		
		Grammar	Grammar technical	Compre-hensive
Successful	Academic orientation	19·27	15·93	18·27
	Motivational awareness	28·27	30·27	26·13
	Hindrance	21·70	18·87	20·80
Achieving as expected	Academic orientation	19·87	16·87	16·67
	Motivational awareness	26·78	27·03	28·13
	Hindrance	21·70	17·53	20·87
Unsuccessful	Academic orientation	17·90	14·50	16·25
	Motivational awareness	28·20	22·45	28·05
	Hindrance	19·78	22·00	17·05
Total	Academic orientation	19·12	15·93	16·91
	Motivational awareness	27·56	26·37	27·65
	Hindrance	21·11	19·22	19·68
F ratios	Schools	Academic orientation	8·36**	
		Motivational awareness	< 1	
		Hindrance	2·28	

Group	Scale	School		
		Grammar	*Grammar technical*	*Compre-hensive*
Success groups	Academic orientation		2·45	
	Motivational awareness		< 1	
	Hindrance		< 1	
Interaction	Academic orientation		1·65	
	Motivational awareness		12·53**	
	Hindrance		12·07**	

Table A7.4 *Number of boys in successful, average and unsuccessful groups in each school*

	Grammar	Grammar technical	Comprehensive	Total
Successful	30	15	15	60
Achieving as expected	60	30	30	120
Unsuccessful	40	20	20	80
Total	130	65	65	260

APPENDIX 5

1 *The love/hostility dimension*

Would you say that - - - - was affectionate when he was a small boy?
In what ways did he show this?
Would you say that - - - - is affectionate now?
In what ways does he show this?
When - - - - is unhappy what do you usually do?
What do you usually do when you see - - - - having difficulties doing something?
Have there been occasions when you have wished that - - - - would ask you for help? When?
How often have you felt that - - - - asks for help unnecessarily?
Ideally, if you could change anything about - - - - at the present time, what would you like to see different?
What are you most proud of in your son? Do you show him how you feel? What do you do?
Do you think - - - - worries about things? What about?
How do you know he is worrying?

2 *The autonomy/control dimension*

Have you ever been worried about any of the friends that - - - -
    has made?
If yes, when was this? Why were you worried?
Did you take any action?
If yes, what action?
How did - - - - react to this?
Has - - - - ever wanted to grow his hair long?
If yes, when was this?
Did you take any action?
If yes, what action?
How did - - - - react to this?
Do you have any rules about the times he can watch TV?
If yes, what are they?
What do you do if he disobeys?
How does he react to the rules?
Do you have any rules about the programmes he can watch?
If yes, what are they?
What do you do if he disobeys?
How does he react to the rules?
By what time has he to be in at night during the week? At the
    weekend?
Is it ever any trouble to get him in at that time?
What do you do if he stays out late?
Does he ever answer back?
Has he always been like this?
What do you do when this happens?
Have you always done this?
Is it ever any trouble to get him to do his homework?
If yes, how often?
Do you take any action to see that homework is done?
If yes, what do you do?
What happens if he disobeys?
Where does he usually do his homework?
Who else is usually with him? What are they doing?
Does he ever do it anywhere else?
How long does his homework usually take him?
Does it ever take more or less time than that?

3 *Methods of control*

What sort of things do you try to encourage in - - - -?

How do you do this?

Did you use the same kind of encouragement when he was a little boy? If no, what did you use?

What kind of behaviour in - - - - do you regard as very bad?

What do you do when he behaves like that?

What else do you do when he is naughty or misbehaves?

How often do you have to do this? What do you do it for?

Did you use the same punishments when - - - - was a little boy? If not, what did you use?

Have you ever smacked - - - -? Have you had to smack him in the past year?

Looking back, which do you think works best with - - - -, reward or punishment?

APPENDIX 6

Linkage analysis is the simplest of all methods of clustering. 'It classifies all variables, no matter how fallible, into an internally consistent and exacting hierarchical structure without at the same time determining the kind of structure; the data themselves determine the kind of structure, and the results indicate whether the structure is dimensional or typal. Linkage analysis is therefore widely appropriate.'[1]

The procedure used was a modification of McQuitty's method[2] in which the steps are as follows:

(i) Find the highest entry in a matrix; it mediates between two variables i and j, representing two columns and two rows

(ii) Combine i and j into a single variable ij to be used in forming a new column and row

(iii) Determine the entries in every cell of column (and row) ij by taking the mean correlation of i and j with every variable in the matrix

(iv) Drop rows and columns i and j to yield a matrix identical

[1] McQuitty L. L. (1964), 'Capabilities and improvements of linkage analysis as a clustering method', *Education and Psychological Measurement* xxiv (3), p. 441.
[2] ibid., p. 442.

with the one of step (i) above except that columns and
rows *i* and *j* have been replaced by column and row *ij*

(v) This process is repeated until all the correlation coefficients
have dropped below the level of significance

(vi) The results of this diminution of the number of variables
in the matrix is then recorded in the form of a diagram
which has as its vertical axis the number of hierarchical
levels and as its horizontal axis the variables of the matrix.
The linkages between the variables are then shown at the
appropriate level.

APPENDIX 7

CONTROLLED ABILITY SAMPLE

It will be recalled that the sample of pupils in each of the schools was drawn from a different level of the ability range as measured by the 11-plus quotient scores and teachers' estimates. From Table 1.1 on page 8, it will be seen, however, that there is some degree of overlap in the three schools. The pupils in the lower range of the grammar school have the same total 11-plus quotient score as the top pupils in the comprehensive school.

Cut-off points at the top and bottom of this range (total quotient scores of 735 and 650 respectively) were therefore fixed. Within these limits, it could be said that pupils of a similar level of ability in each of the schools were represented.

In order that the variable of social class should be controlled, all the boys from middle-class and single-parent homes were excluded. This gave a sample of working-class children whose 11-plus quotient scores fell within the specified limits – 52 in the traditional grammar school, 63 from the technical grammar school and 22 from the comprehensive school.

Within the specified limits of the 11-plus quotient range, the distribution of the sample within each of the schools reflected the overall distribution of 11-plus scores of the pupils in the three schools. Thus in the grammar school the distribution was skewed towards the top end of the range and in the comprehensive school the distribution was skewed towards the bottom end of the range. This degree of skewedness was reflected in the mean scores of the controlled ability samples in each of the schools. The mean score of the sample from the grammar school was highest, the technical grammar school intermediate and the comprehensive school lowest.

Parental sample

In order to obtain information on the home background of the boys in the controlled ability sample, a number of parents were randomly selected for interview in each school. For this purpose boys from middle-class homes were included.

INDEX